Ice Cream Joe
The Valley Dairy Story

May all your days be flavorful!

Joe Mascoli
(Ice Cream Joe) 2006

Ice Cream Joe
The Valley Dairy Story

AND AMERICA'S LOVE AFFAIR WITH ICE CREAM

General Editor

Richard David Wissolik, Ph.D., Fellow of the Center

Editors

Joseph E. Greubel, Fellow of the Center
Virginia Greubel
Barbara Wissolik, Fellow of the Center
Katie Killen, Fellow of the Center
Srdan Smailbegovich, Fellow of the Center
Marianne Vaczi, Fellow of the Center
Don Orlando

Design Editor

Michael Cerce, Fellow of the Center
Downs and Associates

PUBLICATIONS OF THE SAINT VINCENT COLLEGE
CENTER FOR NORTHERN APPALACHIAN STUDIES
2004

Publications of the Saint Vincent College
Center for Northern Appalachian Studies

Saint Vincent College
300 Fraser Purchase Road
Latrobe, PA 15650

www.stvincent.edu
Special Programs
Center for Northern Appalachian Studies
rwissolik@stvincent.edu

Ice Cream Joe is a registered trademark.
All rights reserved. No portion of this publication may be
reproduced, stored in a retrieval system, or transmitted, in any form or by any
means, electronic, mechanical, or otherwise, without prior written
permission from Valley Dairy and the
Saint Vincent College Center for Northern Appalachian Studies.

**Ice Cream Joe©:
The Valley Story...
And America's Love Affair With Ice Cream**

General Editor
Richard David Wissolik
Editors
Joseph E. Greubel   Srdan Smailbegovich
Virginia Greubel   Marianne Vaczi
Barbara Wissolik   Don Orlando
Katie Killen
Design Editor
Michael Cerce

Printed in the United States of America
by Sheridan Books, Ann Arbor, MI

Library of Congress Cataloging-in-Publication Data

Ice Cream Joe : the Valley Dairy story— : and America's love affair with ice cream /
general editor, Richard David Wissolik ; editors, Joseph E. Greubel ... [et al.].
  p. cm.
  ISBN 1-885851-18-9
  1. Ice cream parlors—Pennsylvania—History. 2. Valley Dairy—History. I. Wissolik,
Richard David, 1938– II. Greubel, Joseph E. III. St. Vincent College. Center for Northern
Appalachian Studies.

TX795.I26 2004
381'.4174'09748—dc22

2004052337

In Memoriam

Joseph Fleming Greubel
"Ice Cream Joe"
1913 – 1991

Joseph F. Greubel ("Ice Cream Joe"), Chairman of the Board and founder of Valley Dairy, died suddenly at his home on July 1, 1991.

"Ice Cream Joe" started the Valley Dairy business operation in 1938 with the opening of the first store in Latrobe, Pennsylvania. The road was not an easy one, but he believed in working hard and making any sacrifice necessary for the good of the business. He worked long hours and endured lean times.

"Quick, Friendly Service, Correct Portions, Sensible Prices," was his business creed, and he printed it on a sign that hung in that first store.

Joe Greubel started the ice cream division of the business in the first store. He made ice cream by hand in the kitchen after store hours. He applied the same discipline, perseverance, and business sense to the ice cream business, and now Valley Dairy has its own plant in Windber, Pennsylvania. Today, that plant supplies ice cream and related products to Valley Dairy restaurants as well as local supermarkets, institutional food distributors, and other area ice cream distributors.

Joe Greubel believed in people; he was a mentor to many. He was proud of all the people who got their first jobs at Valley Dairy. It was a pride that extended to those who stayed and those who went on to other, successful careers. Joe Greubel believed in serving the public. He made that a part of this his work. He was practical, yet many of his ideas were ahead of their time. His fame extended beyond the local area. He truly was the legendary "Ice Cream Joe," a character that has given him certain immortality.

We miss him, but we will never forget him. As the business he founded continues to grow, we will all be saying, "Good, Ice Cream Joe," for a good, long time.

It is to the memory of Joseph F. Greubel that this book is lovingly dedicated.

TABLE OF CONTENTS

"Howdy Folks": A Foreword by Joseph E. Greubel ix

"Ask Joe Greubel": A Note by Michael Turback xi

Where Did It All Begin: America's Love Affair With Ice Cream 1

Valley Dairy: The First Twenty Years 17

Joseph F. Greubel: The "Real" Ice Cream Joe 27

Merrily We Roll Along: The Legendary Ice Cream Joe 51

Bryce Thomson: The World's Greatest Soda Jerk 71

The Great American Banana Split Controversy 87

Patrons 103

Promoting the Product 117

Remembering the Magic 157

The Last Dip 167

Acknowledgements 190

Sources and Bibliography 195

Foreword

Joseph Edward Greubel
"Ice Cream Joe"
President of Valley Dairy

"Howdy Folks!"

Somewhere between "You bet your boots," "Howdy folks," and "Hi, Neighbor" is Ice Cream Joe, The Valley Dairy Story. The time frame spans over 100 years and includes a cast of family, friends, customers, employees, and vendors, both living and dead, and too numerous to count. Some stories may remain memories and never make it to print. People, aware or unaware of this book's publication may have missed an opportunity to tell theirs. Some may have preferred to cherish special memories privately.

When great-grandpa Joseph A. Greubel came to the United States from Germany, the first English words he learned were "You bet your boots!" He had heard this phrase at the boat docks, and it was his first response to any question. I knew him by the stories Dad told me, stories about how hard he worked and how he was the first person to manufacture ice cream commercially in Westmoreland County. Later in my life I took a trip to Germany. There I was able to learn more about great-grandpa and our family from Richard and Alwin Kreher. I was also able to visit the 200-year-old Ziegler house in Münster, the home of great-grandpa's first wife, Carolina Ziegler.

"Howdy folks," is from the Ice Cream Joe, street-vending era, which lasted from 1947 until 1954. It was a wonderful time in my life, because I got to go on many business trips with Dad. We always had a great time together, and some of those years are my fondest memories, which will be shared with you in these pages. Ice Cream Joe franchise dealers operated in Western Pennsylvania, Ohio, and West Virginia. Ice Cream Joe became so popular with the kids, that he was second only to Santa Claus.

"Hi, neighbor," was Dad's way of greeting people. He knew so many of them by face, if not by name. From the time of his first Valley Dairy in 1938 on Main Street in Latrobe, Pennsylvania, he loved his customers and showered them with quick, friendly service.

Dad touched a lot of lives. He loved work, he loved people, and he had a great desire to be successful. Helping people was such a natural trait in him, and he could not resist trying to make them thrifty in the process.

A special thanks to all who have contributed to this book. It's my hope that anyone who has been part of the Ice Cream Joe/Valley Dairy story will take pride in this publication. It's a tribute in which we can all share.

Joseph E. Greubel
Son of Ice Cream Joe
Latrobe, Pennsylvania
March 2004

"Ask Joe Greubel"

Michael Turback
Food Historian, Author,
Founder of
icecreamsundae.com

Like so much of history, even ice cream begins with the ancient Romans. Emperor Nero Claudius Caesar (54–68 AD) is said to have sent teams of slave runners to the mountains to bring snow and ice to cool and freeze the earliest frozen dessert. He would flavor the snow with honey, juices, and fruit pulp — a preview of ice cream sundaes to come.

By 96 AD, the Romans had completed their colonization of the Rhineland and regions of the Mosel and the Danube. It is all but certain that their sophisticated eating and drinking habits influenced the Germans, and, by the nineteenth century, ice cream was common in Germany's largest cities. In the wave of German immigration, America inherited not only some of the best brewers and bakers, but also many of the best ice cream makers from the homeland. Among our country's most influential ice cream pioneers are names such as Breyer, Dreyer, Graeter, and Greubel.

Joseph A. Greubel, a young German immigrant, was the first ice cream entrepreneur in Pennsylvania's Westmoreland County, providing delivery by horse and buggy as far back as 1884. His grandson, Joseph F. Greubel, known as "Ice Cream Joe," opened the first Valley Dairy in 1938 in Latrobe, Pennsylvania. Today, the Greubel family enterprise of ice cream parlors and restaurants is operated by Joseph E. Greubel, and his wife and daughters, Virginia, Melissa, and Mary Jo.

I was lucky enough to meet Joe Greubel when I was writing my first book *A Month of Sundaes*. Later, while conducting research for *The Banana Split Book*, Joe helped me tell the story of Latrobe's gift to the world. Whenever I asked someone in Latrobe for more information about Dr. David Strickler and the Banana Split Sundae he invented in 1904, they told me to "ask Joe Greubel." Joe cherishes his friendship with the late fellow Pitt alum, the father of America's greatest dessert, and he carries on a tradition that has lasted over a century.

I tip my soda jerk cap to Joe Greubel. He is quite a guy, with quite a story to tell. It pleases me to introduce you to the tasty and joyful story of "Ice Cream Joe," his contribution to the American ice cream industry, Valley Dairy, and one family's American Dream come true. It is well written, readable, and entertaining for anyone interested in ice cream or history or both.

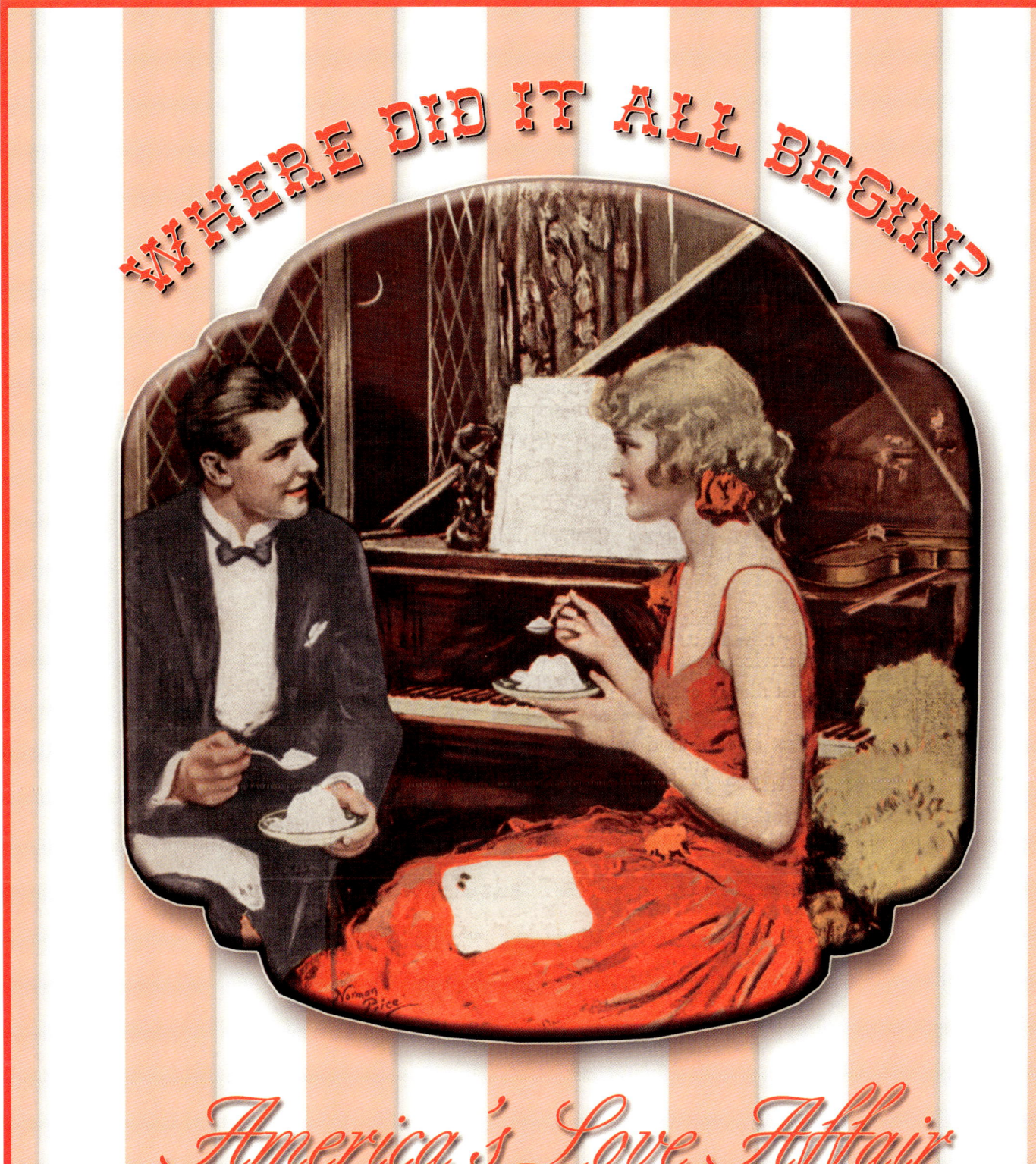

WHEN DID IT ALL BEGIN?

Theories concerning the early invention of ice cream abound. Nearly all of them are apocryphal, the stuff of myth and legend.

Though no one knows for sure when ice cream was "invented," it is probably safe to say that humans experimented with frozen desserts (if nature was kind enough to provide a handy source of snow and ice) even before recorded history. After all, it wouldn't have taken much genius to figure out that honey, fruits, wines, and whatever other sweetening agents might have been available would make the fluffy, white stuff taste good.

Greeks, Romans (notably the Emperor Nero), Hebrews, Alexander the Great, Richard the Lion Heart have all been credited with producing or commissioning some form of frozen concoction. None, it seems, went beyond what were simple frozen drinks.

Emperor Nero on a Roman coin

The ancient and medieval Chinese, who are said to have invented gunpowder, paper, ink, fireworks and pasta, have been credited also with the invention of ice cream, as long ago as 1100 BC.

Various writers claim that these ancient Chinese left accounts, which mention frozen, flavored milk foods, but none include any real documentation.

Perhaps the myth of Chinese origin stems from recorded fact that they had found a way to conserve winter ice in icehouses, kept cool by evaporation. The Shih Ching, a collection of food poetry written around 1100 BC, says:

In the days of the second month, [of the summer festival] they hew out the ice . . . in the third month they convey it to the ice houses which they open in those of the fourth, early in the morning, having offered in sacrifice a lamb with scallions.

In the thirteenth century, the Italian explorer (revisionists say he was really of Slavic descent) Marco Polo is said to have brought the knowledge of ice cream making to Italy on his return from China (he also brought the knowledge of pasta making from the same place, so they say).

In his account *Description of the World*, Polo comments that in China he saw "...milk dried into a kind of paste." From this the legend grew that what he saw was ice cream. It is more likely, however, that what he really saw was some species of yogurt.

Ice cream, as we know it today, is absolutely an Italian invention. It was a common dish at the court of the Medici family in Florence. When Catherine de Medici traveled to France to marry Henry, Duc D'Orleans (later King Henry II), she took along with her several of her chefs and their ice cream recipes. Catherine and Henry celebrated their union for a solid month, during which time they served guests different ice cream flavors, including lemon, orange, cherry, and strawberry.

Catherine de Medici

Ice Cream Joe: THE VALLEY DAIRY STORY

The delicacy was not, however, shared with the general population. Catherine's recipes were jealously guarded, to be enjoyed only by members of the Royal estate. In little more than one hundred years later, another Italian named Procopio would bring ice cream to the French public.

After Catherine de Medici, references to ice cream abound in the literature.

In England, King Charles I (1600-1649) generously paid his French chef, de Mirco, to produce "crème ice" exclusively for the king's table, keeping the recipe secret. Charles lost his head to the executioner in 1649, after which, so goes the tale, de Mirco sold the secret recipe to some noblemen.

King Charles I of England
Anthony Van Dyck's Portrait.

In 1671, with the English monarchy restored, King Charles II, the beheaded Charles' son, served "iced cream" at Windsor Castle in honor of the feast of England's patron, Saint George. Only those privileged to sit at the king's table got the rare dessert.

During the reign of Louis XIV of France (1638-1715), a court confectioner, L. Audiger, became famous for his creative frozen desserts. A guest at one of Louie's spectacular banquets describes one such concoction:

"Toward the end of the feast, his chef caused to be placed before each guest, in silver gilt cups, what was apparently a freshly laid egg, colored like those of Easter, but before the company had time to recover from their surprise at such a novelty at dessert, they discovered that the supposed eggs were delicious sweetmeats, cold and compact as marble. King Louie's renowned chef, Vatel, served a frozen dish also in the shape of an egg. He called it the "'Strawberry Bomb.'"

For many years, ice cream remained the exclusive dish of royalty and the rich, until, that is, the Sicilian, Franceso Procopio, opened a still-existing café in Paris on Rue Fossés-Saint Germain (dare we call it a soda fountain?) Procopio sold a variety of flavors of ice cream and sherbet to the people of Paris.

By the middle of the eighteenth century, people on both sides of the Atlantic were eating ice cream, though it still remained a rare item among the common folk.

In Virginia, William Black recorded in his *Journal* (1744) the first reference to ice cream in America. After dinner at the Maryland governor's mansion, Black wrote:

> [Then] came a Dessert no less Curious; Among the Rarities of which it was Compos'd, was some fine Ice Cream which, with the Strawberries and Milk, eat most deliciously.

In Paris (1768), a person named Emy published *The Art of Making Frozen Dessert*. Emy called ice cream "a food for the gods."

In New York (1774), the chef and caterer, Phillip Lenzi, advertised in a newspaper that he had just traveled from London and would offer ice cream to his clients.

Plantation owners in the American south kept icehouses near riverbanks, in which they stored blocks of winter ice shipped from New England. The icehouses were accessible through tunnels. Slaves hauled the ice through the tunnels, but it was the master's family and friends who enjoyed cool drinks, ice cream, and iced delicacies through the summers.

Thomas Jefferson's meticulously copied recipe for vanilla ice cream, his favorite flavor. Courtesy: Library of Congress.

In 1782, George Washington ate ice cream at a Philadelphia gathering hosted by the French minister. Washington also ate ice cream served by Alexander Hamilton's wife, Elizabeth. This was in 1789. Washington developed a typical addiction to the confection, and served it weekly at presidential dinners. It wasn't long before he bought his own "cream machine for ice" to be used at his estate, Mount Vernon. Washington must have eaten lots of ice cream. According to the ledgers of a New York store, Washington spent upwards of $200.00 for ice cream in the summer of 1790.

Washington was not alone among the Founding Fathers to have developed a taste for ice cream. Thomas Jefferson not only ate it, but, after his fashion, became an authority on its making and a commentator on its virtues. Jefferson, while president, copied the recipes of his chef, and took them back to his estate at Monticello. In his notebooks he observed: "Snow gives the most delicate flavor to creams, but ice is the most powerful congealer and lasts longer." Like Washington, Jefferson obtained his own "cream machine for ice," which he obtained while serving in France. The machine was called a *sorbetiere*.

Jefferson served ice cream at the White House. A guest described one dessert as, "Ice cream, quite good, crust wholly dried, crumbled into thin flakes." Another guest described the same dessert as, "Ice-cream brought to the table in the form of small balls, enclosed in cases of warm pastry." Perhaps this was a prototype of Baked Alaska, as some historians have said. Jefferson was especially partial to vanilla.

In 1794, French gourmand, Authelme Brittat-Savarin, described how one Captain Collet sold ice cream in New York, and the looks on the faces of women as they ate the confection:

Nothing could be more amusing than the little grimaces they make when eating... they were utterly at a loss to conceive how a substance could be kept so cold in a temperature of ninety degrees.

In the early 1800s, Philadelphia became the ice cream capital of the United States because of how much cream it produced in its several ice cream "factories." A popular flavor was Vanilla Egg, named "The Philadelphia."

A freed slave from Delaware, "Aunt Sally" Shadd, was honored among the African-American population as the inventor of ice cream. In her catering business she featured the "new" dessert made from frozen cream, sweeteners, and various fruits. Dolly Madison, wife of President James Madison, heard about Aunt Sally. As things went, Aunt Sally catered her ice cream at Madison's second Inaugural Ball (1813). Thereafter, ice cream became the "official" White House dessert.

Dolly Madison.
Gilbert Stuart Portrait Courtesy: Philadelphia Museum of Art

Another African-American, Augustus Jackson, a chef at the White House, resigned his position and left for Philadelphia, where he invented new ice cream flavors and devised new methods of making ice cream. Jackson delivered ice cream in tin cans to Philadelphia's growing number of ice cream parlors. Along the way, Jackson earned the title. "The Father of Ice Cream."

A breakthrough for ice cream came in 1843. In that year, Nancy Johnson (hometown unknown) invented a hand-cranked ice cream freezer (U.S. Patent 3254), the kind used in today's households. After her invention, ice cream would become less of a rare delicacy to be enjoyed by the few who could afford it. Now, anyone would be able to make excellent ice cream at home.

Another ice cream revolution occurred in Baltimore in 1851, when Jacob Fussell, a dairyman, started the first ice cream wholesale business. The enterprising Fussell reduced the price of quart containers of ice cream by a large margin. Today, in Baltimore, at the corner of Hillen and Exeter Streets, there is a memorial that honors Fussell as the founder of the American ice cream industry. "More than anyone else," one historian says, "[Fussell] was responsible for starting the Americans' love affair with ice cream."

After the Civil War, American westward expansion burgeoned. Cities grew as the number of immigrants from Europe dramatically increased. On the ice cream scene appeared the "Hokey-Pokey Men," the ice cream street vendors, a phenomenon that had its origins in England. In America, the early Hokey-Pokey Men were appropriately of Italian descent, and they sold their confections as they called out *Ecco un poco* 'try a sample.' Children were especially attracted to the Hokey Pokey Men. Since the vendors' sanitary standards were low, parents chastised their children for being attracted to their wares.

Jacob Fussell.

The ice cream vendors would shout:

> Hokey-pokey, pokey ho. Hokey-pokey, a penny a lump. Hokey-pokey, find a cake; hokey-pokey on the lake. Here's the stuff to make you jump; hokey-pokey, penny a lump. Hokey-pokey, sweet and cold; for a penny, new or old.

Ragged children on New York City's Bowery buy from a Hokey-Pokey Man. The accompanying 1901 article says, "Thriftless, but affectionate, is the lower class parent. Shoes the child must do without. But here is five cents to buy hokey-pokey." Bettman Archive.

In 1884, Joseph A. Greubel, a German immigrant, started the first commercially produced ice cream industry in Derry (Westmoreland County) Pennsylvania. His grandson, Joseph F. Greubel, would eventually become the legendary Ice Cream Joe.

In 1897, A.L. Cralle, an African-American inventor from Pittsburgh, obtained U.S. Patent 576,395, for an Ice Cream Mold and Disher (a scoop), a device that prevented sticking and could be used with one hand. Cralle's original design is still recognizable today. Shortly thereafter, in 1899, August Gaulin, a Frenchman, invented the homogenizer, a device, which breaks down the fat in ice cream, and gives it the smoothness we have come to appreciate.

Into the twentieth century, electricity, innovations in freezing techniques and refrigeration revolutionized the ice cream industry. From 1899 to 1919, ice cream consumption in the United States increased from thirty million gallons to 150 million. The use of dry ice extended the shelf life of ice cream. In 1902, another Frenchman, August Gaulin, invented the brine freezer, which allowed for faster freezing.

In 1904, Dr. David Strickler, a clerk at Tassel's Drug Store in Latrobe, Pennsylvania, invented the banana split, as we know it - vanilla, chocolate, strawberry ice cream and the trimmings. Dr. Strickler also designed the traditional, elongated banana-split dish, which a glass factory in Grapeville, Pennsylvania produced for him.

Also, in 1904, at the St. Louis World's Fair, Ernest Hamwi, an immigrant from Syria, was selling thin waffle cakes. The ice cream vendor next to him ran out of dishes. Hamwi quickly shaped some of his waffles to hold ice cream. Hamwi is generally credited with inventing the first ice cream cone, but that he did so is disputed. Edible cones are documented in Mrs. Agnes Marshall's 1894 book, *Fancy Ices*.

In 1926, Clarence Vogt, an inventor from Louisville, Kentucky, created the first, successful continuous-process freezer. The mass production of ice cream was on its way.

Twelve years later, J.F. (Grandpa) McCullough and Alex McCullough invented soft-serve ice cream, thus giving birth to Dairy Cream. J.F. served his ice cream before it was frozen into its final form. He thought that, in its soft stage, ice cream tasted better. The McCulloughs obtained a frozen-custard machine from Chicago, held a sale ("All You Can Eat for Ten Cents"), and, in a little over two hours, sold 1,600 servings.

In 1938, Joseph Greubel founded the Valley Dairy chain in Latrobe, Pennsylvania.

Joseph A. Greubel, Sr. and his grandson, three-year-old Joseph Fleming Greubel, the future Ice Cream Joe and founder of the Valley Dairy Restaurant chain. The 1916 photo was taken in front of J.A.'s dry goods and confectionary in Derry, Pennsylvania. The elder Greubel, a German immigrant, started the first commercially produced ice cream industry in Derry (Westmoreland County). Even at that young age, the grandson helped to sell ice cream at the store. In a Greensburg Tribune-Review feature (Sunday, October 16, 1988) Joe is quoted as saying: "I helped out at my grandfather's bakery from the time I was three. By the time I was fifteen I was baking and clerking, delivering ice cream to Idlewild Park and other places, and doing whatever needed to be done."

The photo below was taken in 1938, the year Joe F. Greubel founded the first Valley Dairy store in Latrobe, Pennsylvania. Joe is seen in the center of the photo scooping ice cream for the kids, who are waiting to see Gene Autry's latest feature Mountain Rhythm.
- Greubel Family Archives.

Ice Cream Joe: THE VALLEY DAIRY STORY

TOPPINGS

In Massachusetts, milkshakes have no ice cream. If you want a traditional milkshake, order a "frappe."

In Rhode Island, if you want an ice cream milkshake, order a "cabinet."

During the Victorian period, drinking soda water was considered to be improper, so the practice was banned on Sundays. A druggist in Evanston, Indiana, is said to have invented a legal alternative ice cream and syrup, without soda. To demonstrate respect for the Sabbath, he called it a "Sundae."

Over the years, everything in the soda water business got a nickname. Here are a few: *Belch Water* (Seltzer); *Black Cow* (chocolate ice cream); *Black and White* (vanilla shake with chocolate syrup); *Cow Juice* (milk); *Mud* (chocolate ice cream); *No Cow* (without milk); *Jimmies* (chocolate bits or sprinkles); *Pink Stick* (strawberry ice cream cone).

The biggest ice cream sundae in history was made in Edmonton, Alberta, Canada, in 1988. It weighed in at twenty-four tons.

Thomas Jefferson would be pleased to know that the most popular ice cream flavor is still vanilla.

The most popular topping for ice cream is chocolate syrup.

July is "National Ice Cream Month."

The third Sunday in July is "National Ice Cream Day."

Some types of ice cream use "carrageenan" to improve texture and thickness. carrageenan is a kind of red seaweed stabilizer.

Which NICRA President was known as "Sheik Sneak A Peek?"

Ice Cream Joe: THE VALLEY DAIRY STORY

Top left: Two fashionable, Manhattan dowagers cool off with their ice cream cones. Right: Ice cream eaters in a Philadelphia ad of the nineteenth century. Everything needed for their culinary enjoyment is at the ready. Apparently, the ice cream making itself was performed by an assortment of elves seen bounding in from the upper-left side of the etching. Bottom: Young boys feast on ice cream and puff on cigars. The ad is an attempt by moralists to decry the evils of ice cream and tobacco. - Bettman Archive.

Ice Cream Joe: THE VALLEY DAIRY STORY

The Penny-Ice Man

In summer when the sun is high,
    And children's lips are parched and dry,
An ice is just the thing to try.
So this young man who comes, 'tis plain,
    From Saffron Hill or Leather Lane,
A store of pence will quickly gain.
"A lemon ice for me," says Fred;
    Cries Sue, "No, have a cream instead."
"A raspberry!" shouts Newsboy Ned.
"What fun! Although we're now in June,
    It feels"—says Ned—"this afternoon,
Like eating winter with a spoon!"

Early illustrations and a photograph of Hokey-Pokey men. Concerned members of the public and civic officials questioned the sanitary conditions under which they delivered their treats. A glance at the containers in the photo below testifies to the fact that they had good cause for concern.
- Bettman Archive.

THE HOKEY POKEY MAN

Ice Cream Joe: THE VALLEY DAIRY STORY

A 1974 Boucher photo of a Tiffany lamp from Zaharaka's soda fountain installed when the establishment opened in Columbus, Indiana, in 1900. Library of Congress.   Inserts: After Tufts introduced his two-story, elaborately designed soda fountain at the Philadelphia Centennial in 1876, various companies began to produce equally elaborated counter fountains, catering to the taste of the Victorian Age. The four largest manufactures, Tufts, Puffer, Lippincott and Matthews, merged in 1894 to become the American Soda Fountain Company. - New York Historical Society.

Ice Cream Joe: THE VALLEY DAIRY STORY

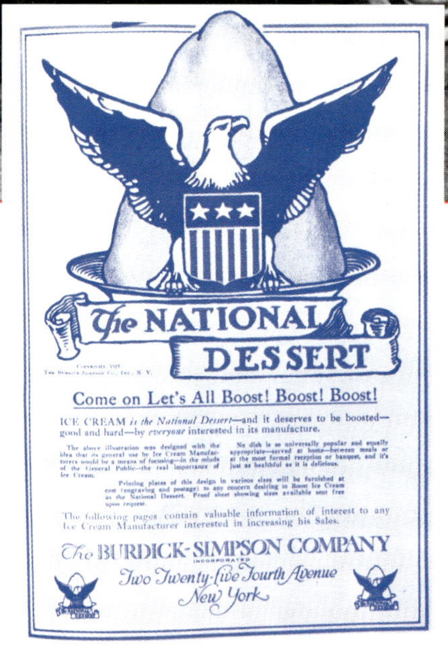

Illustration above: It wasn't long before ice cream became known as the "National Dessert," despite its real historical connections.

At left is an Eskimo Pie representative filling a dry-ice Eskimo Pie dispensing machine. In 1919, Christian Nelson found a way to make chocolate adhere to ice cream. Thus was born the chocolate-covered ice cream bar. Christian first called it the "I-Scream Bar," but later changed the name to "Eskimo Pie."
- Eskimo Pie Corporation.

Ice Cream Joe: THE VALLEY DAIRY STORY

Ice Cream Joe: THE VALLEY DAIRY STORY

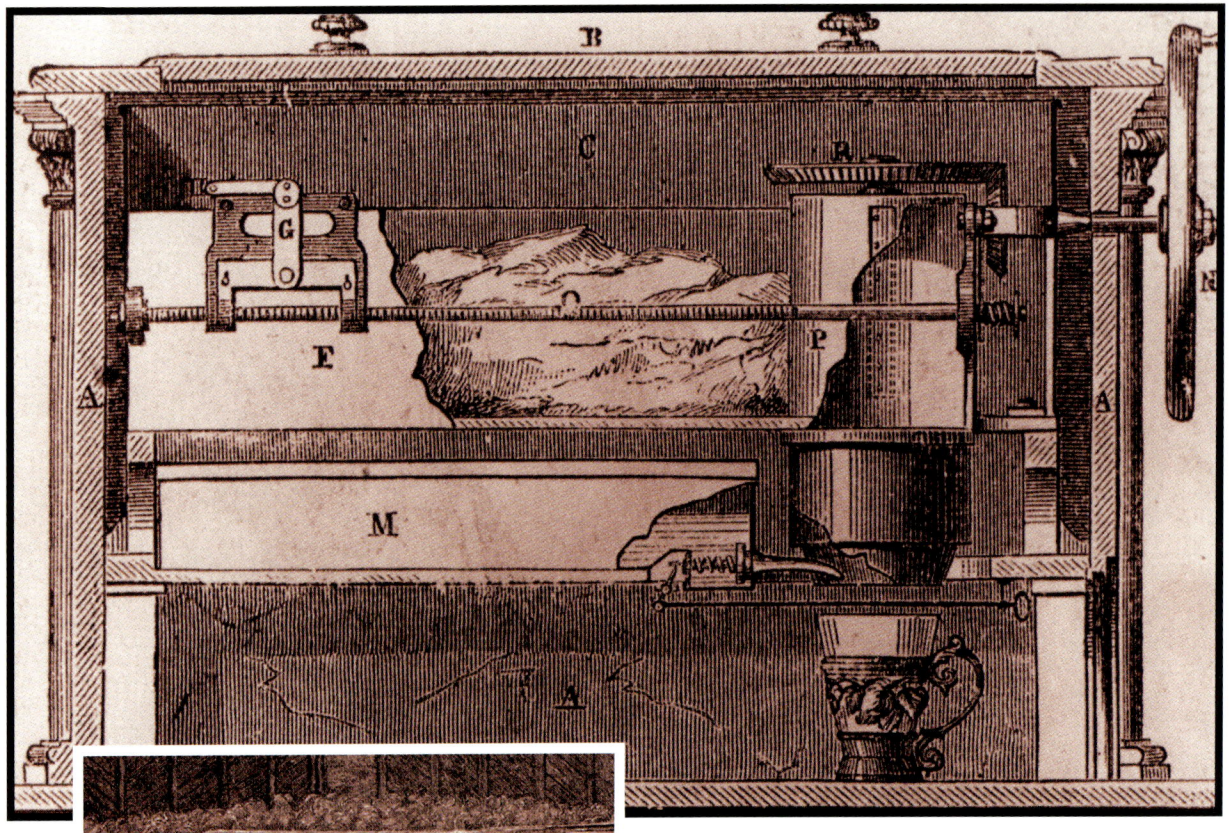

ICE MAKING AND ICE STORAGE FACILITIES OF THE EARLY DAYS

Retrieving ice from a frozen river.

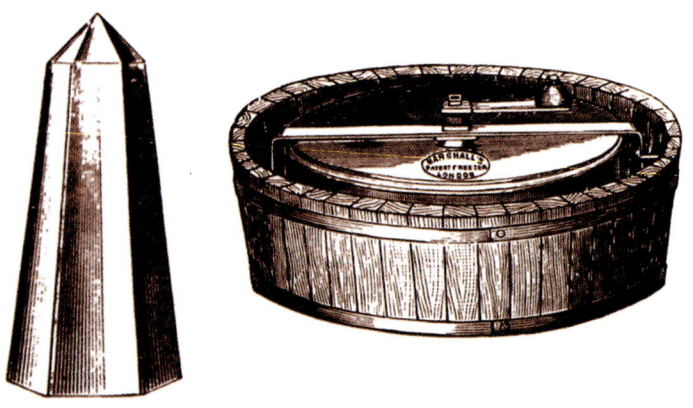

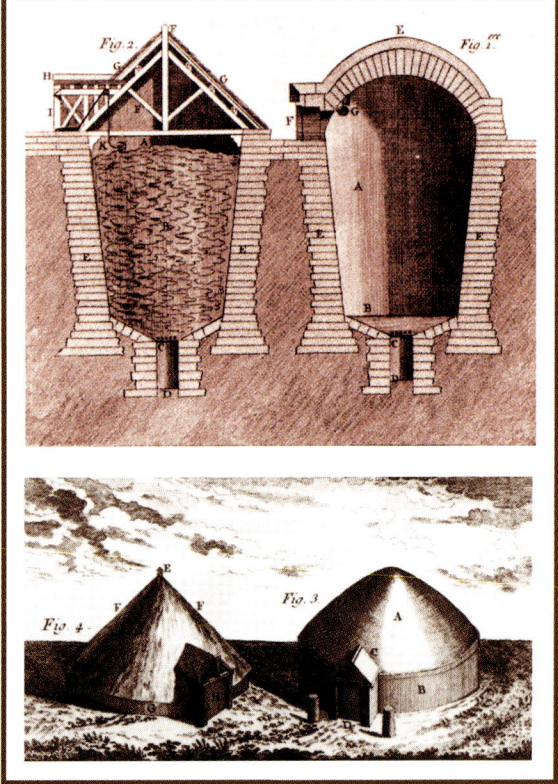

Ice Cream Joe: THE VALLEY DAIRY STORY

TOPPINGS

In 1870, J.M. Horton facilitates ice cream freezing by attaching a steam boiler to a freezer. Joseph A. Greubel began his ice cream retail business using Horton's system. By the 1890s, electricity powers ice cream freezers.

Robert M. Green creates the ice cream soda in 1874 at the semi centennial celebration at Philadelphia's Franklin Institute. James Tufts popularized the soda in 1876 at the Philadelphia Centennial. Crowds gathered to marvel at Tufts's two-story soda fountain.

By 1910, the soda fountain is already a fixture in America. Chicago alone had 3600 soda fountains.

The ice cream sundae is created in the 1890s.

In 1902 Burr Walker of the I.X.L. Ice Cream Company in Warren, Pennsylvania, invented the "brine" freezer, ushering in the age of mechanical refrigeration, and eventually relieving small manufacturers of their dependence on fickle ice supplies and fluctuating salt prices. As use of the brine freezer, and its many improved versions spread, ice cream manufacturing and sales skyrocketed. The ice cream industry would be changed forever.

In 1904, Ernest A. Hamwi, a Syrian who ran a concession stand at the St. Louis World's Fair, is credited with the invention of the edible ice cream cone. Hamwi sold thin, waffle pastries next to an ice cream vendor, who, one day, ran out of dishes. Hamwi immediately rolled one of his "waffles" into the shape of a cone and filled it with ice cream. The claim for Hamwi is greatly disputed, but whoever did invent the cone greatly advanced the popularity of ice cream in the food culture of America.

In 1904, Dr. David Strickler created an ice cream dish in Tassell's Pharmacy in Latrobe, Pennsylvania. Like the ice cream cone, his banana split and banana split dish would become part of American food culture.

By 1911, ice cream is being transported more and more by motor vehicles. By 1919, the era of the horse-drawn delivery wagon comes to a virtual end. Soon, the industry would undergo another significant change when the motor truck is equipped with mechanical or dry ice refrigeration.

In 1913, the first ice cream "vending" machine is introduced at Horn and Hardart's Automat in New York City. Patrons could drop a nickel into a slot, and out would come a dish of ice cream.

In 1923, another "revolutionary" item is introduced by the ice cream industry — the Popsicle, or "The Drink on a Stick." Originally called the "Epsicle," it is the invention of of Californian, Frank Epperson. Other "sicles" follow in quick succession — the fudgesicle and the creamsicle.

Also in 1923, the most famous of all "cupped" ice creams is introduced. The Weed Ice Cream Company of Allentown, Pennsylvania, packages a quarter pint of ice cream in a cup. Eventually, they are called the "Dixie Sundae," or the "Dixie Cup." In 1919, the company begins to put pictures on the underside of the cup tops. By the 1930s, movie stars appeared on the lids, and during World War II, military images appear on the lids together with the stars.

In 1931, I.C. Parker introduces the "Drumstick."

The 1930s see the birth of retail ice cream chains, and wholesale manufacturers create their own controlled outlets. Valley Dairy is one of these.

By the 1950s, Americans see the demise of the soda fountain, and the rise of the supermarket and "dipping" counter. Supermarkets provide self-serve units that contained all varieties of packaged ice cream, while dipping counters in malls offered scores of ice cream flavors. As the day of the soda fountain passes, so does an important part of American culture. The "Drugstore Cowboy" metamorphoses into the "Mall Rat."

Ice Cream Joe: THE VALLEY DAIRY STORY

TOPPINGS

Most, if not all people can taste four flavors: sweet, sour, bitter, and salt. But the greatest of these is "sweet," or so say gourmands. Who doesn't look forward to dessert?

Radio in the 1940s had a "Popsicle Parade of Stars." Milton Berle, Martha Ray, Arthur Godfrey, Fanny Brice, and Fred Allen were among featured celebrities. One night, Milton Berle told the following joke: "There was a cannibal chief who had a sweet tooth. For dessert, he always has a Good Humor Man."

During World War II, in addition to making dehydrated ice cream, the military attempted to put ice cream in cans. The dehydrated stuff had some success with the troops. The canned product did not.

What's in an ice cream flavor? When Dwight Eisenhower was president he had six quarts of borscht ice cream delivered to the White House for a dinner with Russian Premier, Nikita Kruschev. Richard Nixon served Baked Alaska to Leonid Brezhnev who called it "hot ice cream."

A typical diplomatic lunch in the old Soviet Union consisted of a Vodka appetizer, caviar, smoked fish, cold meat, and fish, steak. Ice cream was the dessert. It would be washed down with wine and champagne. One wonders whether an afternoon work session was possible?

There was once an epic film about a soda jerk. The film was called Fighting Blood, and starred one George O'Hare, a soda jerk who becomes a world champion boxer, then makes a fortune selling a concoction he invented as when he worked the fountain.

VALLEY DAIRY

1938-1958

THE FIRST TWENTY YEARS

FAIRVIEW DAIRY AND VALLEY DAIRY, 1938 – 1958
AN AMERICAN DREAM COME TRUE

There's a song that goes something like, "How can your dreams come true, if you don't dream?" Joseph Fleming Greubel certainly knew the answer to that question! Joe was a dreamer, to be sure, but he also understood that dreams were not enough. If he wanted his dream to come true, he knew he had to work hard to make it so.

Shortly after he started his first store, Joe Greubel jotted the following comments on a slip of paper. In them, he tells of his dream and his pledge to the public he will come to serve:

> My goal — January 1, 1940 – January 1, 1960. By the first day of January 1960, I will have in my possession at least $100,00.00, which will come to me in various amounts from time to time during the interim, and also at that time my monthly income will be in excess of $1,000.00. In return for this money, I will give the most efficient service of which I am capable. Rendering the fullest quantity and the best possible quality of service in my capacity of managing Fairview Dairy, Inc. I believe I will achieve my goal, and the monetary amounts herein stated, because my faith is so strong. I will follow my plan each and every day until my goal has been achieved.

Joe kept a personal scrapbook. At the heading of each page is the phrase, "You can do it if you believe you can." On the second page he wrote:

> I fully realize that no wealth or position can long endure unless they are built upon truth and justice. Therefore, I will engage in no transaction that does not benefit all whom it affects. I will eliminate hatred, envy, jealousy, selfishness and cynicism by developing a love for all humanity, because I know that a negative attitude toward others can never bring me success. I will induce others to serve, but I will first serve them. I will cause others to believe in themselves and me, because I will believe in them and myself.

Joe Greubel carried on a tradition begun by his grandfather, Joseph A. Greubel, who, in 1884, was the first in Western Pennsylvania to manufacture ice cream on a commercial basis. He did so from his bakery in Derry, Pennsylvania.

Kefer's Confectionary and Dairy Store maintained its own aircraft which pilot Raymond Elder (seated on wing) flew during airshows at the J.D. Hill Airport (now Arnold Palmer Regional Airport) in Latrobe. One sunny day, local residents were puzzled by a strange rain. They finally discovered that the rain was caused by ice melting in the aircraft.

On October 1, 1938, Greubel, with a personal savings of $500.00 and an unsecured business loan of $2000.00 from a local bank, purchased Kefer's Confectionary and Dairy Store at 313 Main Street in Latrobe, Pennsylvania. Greubel changed the name to Valley Dairy Store, an enterprise that would grow into one of the most successful dairy, ice cream, and restaurant chains in America. Eventually, Valley Dairy would become part of its parent company, Fairview Dairy, in Windber, Pennsylvania.

Joe Greubel worked day and night in his store, and, by 1940, he paid off his original $2,000.00 loan. Utilizing his profits and savings, Joe made improvements to his original store, and purchased equipment and fixtures from a Jeannette, Pennsylvania, dairy store that had gone out of business. On October 23, 1942, Joe opened Valley Dairy #2 at 1419 Ligonier Street in Latrobe, and installed his newly purchased used equipment there. October turned out to be a good month for Joe, and on the first of that month, 1944, Joe opened Valley Dairy #3 at 239 Lloyd Avenue, Latrobe, which he moved to another location (124 Lloyd Avenue) on October 3, 1949.

On May 1, 1946, with $50,000.00 authorized capital, Joe purchased a dairy products and ice cream manufacturing plant in Windber, Pennsylvania, and formed the corporation known today as Fairview Dairy, Inc. The stockholders in the new corporation were Joe, John S. Lightcap, Jr., a Latrobe attorney, and Roy C. Moersch. Also that May, Joe opened Valley Dairy store #4 at 123 E. Main Street, Ligonier, Pennsylvania.

It wasn't long after the date of incorporation that Joe, pledging the assets of both Valley Dairy and Fairview Dairy, negotiated a mortgage loan for $35,000.00 with the Irwin Savings and Trust Company, located in Irwin, Pennsylvania, fifteen miles or so from Latrobe. One year later, the partners transferred the mortgage to Latrobe's First National Bank, and increased the debt to $55,000.00.

In 1947, Joe purchased a retail ice cream truck, hoping to increase sales in areas where there were no Valley Dairy stores. To capture the fancy of children, Joe and Roy Moersch created the character, "Ice Cream Joe," whose body was encased in a cup cone and whose head was crowned with ice cream. On April 11, 1950, "Ice Cream Joe" was trade marked under U.S. Certificate Number 523,911, and issued to Joseph F. Greubel.

On December 1, 1950, Joe sold the retail and wholesale dairy and milk business side of the Fairview Corporation, together with all customer accounts, to the Johnstown Sanitary Dairy Company for $10,000.00. Nine years later, on January 1, 1959, Fairview Dairy, Inc., purchased the four Valley Dairy stores from Joe, and Fairview Dairy became the parent company to Valley Dairy Stores.

From January 1951, until April 1954, the key personnel of Fairview concentrated on creating Ice Cream Joe franchises throughout Western Pennsylvania, Ohio, and West Virginia. The task was enormous, and involved a number to activities that were new to Joe and Roy Moersch. No longer faced with the placing of direct, simple ads in local newspapers, Joe and his growing staff had to develop expertise in designing and developing brochures, cartons, refrigerated trucks, premiums and promotions, Kiddies' Clubs, and the like. More than that, they now had to travel extensively, as they contacted prospective franchise dealers in the United States, Canada, and other foreign countries. They also had to work with advertising agencies, which helped create Ice Cream Joe displays at national conventions and expo exhibits. Finally, Joe established thirty-five franchise dealers whose operations would come to involve 150 ice cream trucks, motorcycles, scooters, bicycles, push carts, and a number of stores.

In the post-war years, sales of ice cream in America reached new heights. This should have meant good times for the American soda fountain and the countless neighborhood ice cream parlors that had spread throughout the small towns of the county. But it did not. In the early 1950s, America would see the coming of one-stop supermarkets, suburban malls, and fast-food restaurants that would spell the doom not only of many of the independent ice cream retailers, but generally of all "hometown" businesses from hardware stores to grocery stores.

Fairview Dairy and Valley Dairy would suffer along with them, and Joe, his family and workers, would need to develop new strategies to stay afloat in the market.

1928. The Fairview Dairy building in Windber, Pennsylvania, as it looked then.

On April 1, 1954, faced with reorganization and financial exigency, Joe discontinued all franchise operations, and turned his employees and key personnel to devoting full time to the operations of Fairview Dairy, Inc. He assigned all Ice Cream Joe rights to the Doughnut Corporation of America (DCA Food Industries, Inc.) for $15,000.00, of which DCA, canceling the contract, paid only $8,000.00. On July 1, 1954, Roy Moersch, Fairview's vice-president, resigned to take a position with DCA.

On September 18, 1957, Joe repaid the $55,000.00 loan to the First National Bank of Latrobe (later Mellon National Bank and Trust). During the first few months of 1958, Joe took a mortgage loan in the amount of $30,000.00 with the Windber Trust Company. With the money he made necessary plant improvements to the Fairview plant and to the Valley Dairy stores.

Eventually, Joe Greubel overcame the difficult years. Today, Valley Dairy stores number twelve, and the pledges Joe made to the public in the year that he started his first store remain company policy.

Ice Cream Joe: THE VALLEY DAIRY STORY

An outdoor juke box at the Fairview Dairy Windber plant. The Valley Dairy Store attached to the Windber plant had a goldfish pond and small picnic area in the rear where patrons could enjoy their treats and music.

Ice Cream Joe: THE VALLEY DAIRY STORY

Top: Grand opening day at the Valley Dairy Store in West Latrobe, early 1940s. Robert Greubel, Joe F.'s brother, on the right. Right: Dorothy Uncapher, Henry Wodowski, a driver for Ward's Bread, and Dick Myers.

Bottom: Joe F. at the counter in Valley Dairy #2, 1419 Ligonier Street, Latrobe.

Ice Cream Joe: THE VALLEY DAIRY STORY

Top: Valley Dairy Store at 1419 Ligonier Street, Latrobe.

Center: Valley Dairy #3 in Latrobe on corner of Unity and Lloyd Avenue. The town's Edsel faded into history, but Valley Dairy flourished.

Bottom left: Valley Dairy Store #1. Chris DeLuca (left), Manager.

Bottom right: Manager Eve Albensi serves kids from a modern freezer (ca. 1950s)

Ice Cream Joe: THE VALLEY DAIRY STORY

Stages of the remodeled Fairview Dairy plant in Windber, Pennsylvania, 3200 Graham Avenue. Front, side, and aerial views. Insert: Ray Sheets (left), Plant Manager, with Richard Kreher, Joe E's cousin from Germany, who samples some freshly made Valley Dairy ice cream.

Ice Cream Joe: THE VALLEY DAIRY STORY

Insert: Fairview delivery truck, 1958. Merle Huston, Plant Manager, in the truck.

Scenes from the Windber plant, 1958. A vat containing Jo-Pop mix. Jo-Pops were a frozen water ice made in a 24-mold brine tank. A hot-air fan blew open the bag into which workers placed the confection. Jo-Pops were made in two parts which could be split and shared.

A young Joe E. Greubel packs ice cream into paper containers. The Fairview Dairy plant produced sixty gallons of ice cream per hour on one of the early continuous freezers made by the Cherry-Burrell Corporation.

CORPORATE STAFF

ICE CREAM JOE IN PROGRESS

The Valley Dairy corporate staff at 1562 Mission Road, Latrobe, Pennsylvania. Left to right: Joe E. Greubel, Virginia Greubel, Ray Zottola, Mary Jo Greubel Sell, John Mackey, Lujean Solomon, Dominic Meddis, Becky Schirf, Rhonda Hazlett.

Right: The future Ice Cream Joe? At the moment he is just Ice Cream Alex, Joe E. Greubel's grandson, son of Melissa Greubel Blystone.

"GENERICALLY GOOD"

Valley Dairy Ice Cream:
A Fifty-Second Radio Spot
January 1, 1985

Joe: GOOD! ICE CREAM JOE! THAT'S WHAT THEY CALL ME . . . .

"ICE CREAM JOE" – AND THEY'VE BEEN SAYING 'GOOD' SINCE 1884.

THAT'S WHEN MY GRANDAD BEGAN MAKING VALLEY DAIRY ICE CREAM.

'I' STARTED MAKING IT IN 1938 AND NOW MY SONS MAKE IT.

SO YA SEE – PEOPLE HAVE BEEN SAYING

'GOOD! ICE CREAM JOE!'

FOR A LONG TIME. WHEN SOMEONE ASKS ME –

WHAT'S YOUR 'SECRET' ICE CREAM JOE?

I ALWAYS SAY. . . . THERE'S NO SECRET ABOUT VALLEY DAIRY ICE CREAM –

IT JUST TAKES 'PRACTICE' . . . .

AND MY FAMILY HAS BEEN PRACTICING FOR OVER A HUNDREN YEARS!

I'LL TELL YA – MY BOYS SURE DO COME UP WITH SOME DELICIOUS FLAVORS –

'DIFFERENT' TOO.

BUY AND TRY VALLEY DAIRY ICE CREAM. DO 'YOURSELF' A FLAVOR –

WE ALWAYS HAVE ONE YOU'LL LIKE –

AND I'M SURE THE NEXT TIME I SEE YOU – YOU'RE GONNA SAY THE SAME THING. . .

GOOD! – ICE CREAM JOE!

Words and voice by Bob Trow who was Bob Dog on the Mr. Rogers TV show

WHO IS THE "REAL" ICE CREAM JOE?

[*A note to the reader: There are actually three "Ice Cream Joes." The first was the character created by Joseph F. Greubel, the second was Joseph F. himself, and the third is his son, Joseph E. Greubel, who carries on the Greubel tradition*].

Greensburg Tribune-Review

SUNDAY, OCTOBER 16, 1988
JOE GREUBEL MAKES VISION SWEET SUCCESS

Back shortly after the turn of the century when Tinker, Evers and Chance were the simply amazing double-play combination of the Chicago Cubs, Arnold Palmer, Fred Rogers and Joe Greubel were still decades away from bringing similar degrees of national recognition to Greater Latrobe.

Palmer eventually scored mightily with golf clubs, Rogers became a favorite of children as the gentle Mister Rogers of public television fame, and Greubel's "Ice Cream Joe" was such a successful marketing concept that the television bigshots behind the fledgling Howdy Doody show wanted a piece the action.

Laughs Greubel, "I'm so far behind Arnie and Fred that it isn't even funny."

Greubel, 75, is the founder of the Valley Dairy chain which began at 313 Main St. in Latrobe, and now numbers twelve restaurants throughout western Pennsylvania. Valley Dairy is celebrating its 50th anniversary, the successful vision of a man who didn't find out he preferred to be in business until he found out he didn't care to work for someone else's business.

"I started working at my grandfather's bakery, confectionery and restaurant in Derry when I was 15, baking and clerking and whatever needed done, but I didn't think I was going to stick with it because it took up too many hours," says Greubel. "I wanted a 9-to-5 job so I went to Pittsburgh to the Arthur Young company in 1932 and they sent me and about fifty other guys over to Peabody High School to take this test. Well, I wasn't too good at such tests and I wrote 'I do not know' on a lot of questions."

"But I got an interview."

"They said that even though my grade wasn't particularly good, they liked the fact that I did not lie and that I did not guess. They hired me as a junior accountant and asked me what salary I wanted. I told them I'd work for nothing for a month."

When the tax season ended, so did Greubel's job and he returned to Latrobe and began to work at Latrobe Steel Co., where he remained employed for five years.

"But I kept telling everybody I worked with that I wouldn't be there too long," he recalls.

One of Greubel's sons, Joseph E., company president, says his dad continued to pick up accounting jobs on the side and one of those was in Ligonier, where the Kefer family operated a dairy store, and in Latrobe. "The Kefers told him they'd give him $10 if he could tell them why the Latrobe store was losing money. So he went down there like a customer, observed a few things and came back with a report. They told him that if he was so smart, why didn't he buy the store?"

So he pooled together his own savings – $500 – and a $2,000 loan secured from a local banker – Fred Kuntz of the First National Bank of Derry – willing to take a big chance.

Greubel poured all he had into that store - lived in it in the early days - and later rode the train, the streetcar, or hitchhiked home to Derry.

"I'll tell you, whatever I did, I wouldn't want you guys to have to do," he says.

In 1940, Greubel began to manufacture ice cream in the kitchen of that store at the rate of twenty gallons-per-hour; a humble beginning compared to the more than 600 gallons-per-hour generated today in the firm's Winder manufacturing plant.

His perseverance and business acumen led to success and that translated into expansion when three Valley Dairy stores were added in the 1940s followed that same decade by the purchase of the Fairview Dairy in Winder. The addition of that facility led to the incorporation of Valley Dairy.

Greubel says his grandfather (Joseph A. Sr.) is generally considered to be the first person in that area to manufacture ice cream, which he did in 1884 using a steam engine to drive a belt that turned a five-gallon container inside of a larger round wooden tub packed with ice and salt. Fresh cream was picked up as needed from farms around New Derry and sugar and flavoring were added.

Joseph A. Greubel, Ice Cream Joe's grandfather, who started Westmoreland County, Pennsylvania's, first commercial ice cream manufacturing enterprise in 1884, at his bakery in Derry, Pennsylvania.

Valley Dairy is known, he says, for pursuing new flavors in ice cream and developing ideas and in 1975, it received the Idea of the Year award from Dairy and Ice Cream Field magazine for its sunflower ice cream.

But another market to be tapped in the 1940s was that of on-the-road, point-of-sale delivery and Greubel knew that it would take a vibrant marketing concept to capture the imagination of children.

"We wanted to create a character to use for the vending of our ice cream that would have direct appeal to children and that's when I came up with the Ice Cream Joe character. The idea was to have a character who didn't age. And it's true that his popularity at that time in this area probably made him second only to Santa Claus in recognition with the children."

That symbol – patented in 1947 – became part of the Valley Dairy system, from appearing on the trucks used by franchisees to store menus. Premiums were issued with each purchase and could be redeemed for various merchandise. In August 1952, Ice Cream Joe generated 20,000 requests for premiums.

Recognition became so widespread and instantaneous that television marketers involved with the "Howdy Doody" show (which premiered in December 1947) sought to buy the by-truck merchandising of ice cream to take advantage of the fame that Buffalo Bob, Clarabelle and Howdy Doody were experiencing. Eventually, Greubel says, his interest in franchising delivery systems waned and "I felt a little bit guilty for having neglected my stores" and decided to concentrate on the Valley Dairy stores.

The company sold the rights to the Ice Cream Joe on-the-road merchandising and Howdy Doody and friends soon replaced Ice Cream Joe on the trucks. As it happened, Valley Dairy was able to regain the rights to "Ice Cream Joe" because of a technicality discovered in the sale.

Greubel consequently became "Ice Cream Joe" in-house and recent years have found him in demand at parades, department store celebrations, public service campaigns. How often does one find the chairman of the board popping up in his stores to greet the customers in a bright red-and-white vest and hat?

"I like to walk about the stores meeting people," says Greubel, while his son adds with a smile that "we'd like him to make more appearances but now that he's discovered he enjoys two days off a week. …"

"I'm only just now starting to not think of Valley Dairy," says Ice Cream Joe. "I like to fish locally, like at Keystone or Twin Lakes or Mammoth. I find it very relaxing and I can forget about my problems."

"There were many years when I never took a vacation and I'm not real proud of that. I remember Christmas mornings waking up my sons at 5:30, and they'd unwrap their presents and I'd be off to work." "One year right after World War II, this fella (Earl Hunter) who owned a service station kept bugging me about going on a trip together and finally one day, I just said, 'Ok, let's go,' but I wasn't crazy about going. We (the wives, too) spent five weeks crossing the country by car. What I remember most and liked the best about that trip was that we didn't have any plans; if we came to a city we really liked we just stayed there."

"In Tijuana, we went into a place with a sign that said 'best restaurant in town' but the food was so hot that none of us could eat it."

"Another place, we pulled into a service station and I blew and blew the horn. When I went in, there were four old cronies sitting there playing cards. One said he'd get me gas in a little while. When I asked what time it was, they said they weren't going anyplace so they didn't need to know what time it was. When I asked if there was a restaurant around, they said there was one down the road a piece. We must have driven 100 miles before we found that restaurant," he says with a hearty laugh.

That five-week, 7,000-mile trip to California and back cost him less than $400, he adds.

Greubel has lived in Derry "on the same street" all his life, which he shared with his late wife, Veronica Connolly, whom he married in 1935.

He talks of guys like Joseph Todaro, a supervisor, who has been with the company for 11 years and Robert Rummel, a vice president and Valley Dairy employee for 24 years who started in a Valley Dairy store as a teen-ager.

"I'd like to be remembered as a fella who loved his work and who loved working with people, especially all the young people. When I think of all the young people who worked here and then went on to become successful, I like to think I had some part in that success. It just makes me feel good when I see that they've become priests, ministers, advertising agency owners, doctors, attorneys, businessmen, and teachers and so on."

Maybe Greubel feels an affinity toward young people just getting started because of Kuntz, the "kind-hearted banker" who loaned him money when he had no collateral to post in the middle the Depression era.

When Greubel paid off the loan in 1939, he sent a personal letter to Kuntz expressing his deepest thanks as well as outlining what he hoped would be a successful business future.

Responded Kuntz: "I had as much faith in you as you had in yourself and I know your Dad had also. I think all I did was bolster your courage at times…"

MARGARET GREUBEL MURREN, 2004
"MY GRANDFATHER CALLED ME BUBBLES"

My grandfather called me "Bubbles" when I was a child and, when I became a teenager, he addressed me as "Hey, Friend!" If I had to make Grandpap a modern cartoon character, I would say he is Mr. Crabs from the Sponge Bob Show. He was all about money and business.

The Valley Dairy stores always took in a great deal of change, which was then sorted and rolled in the office. Grandfather would purposely drop coins, and then tell me to clean up the floor. He knew I would find the coins. Whatever I found, I could keep.

From working in the office, I graduated to store work at Valley Dairy #2 on Ligonier Street in Latrobe. Number 2 was in the same building as the main office. I was probably around six or seven, and I had to stand on a pop case to reach the cash register. I filled the candy and gum racks, and made potato salad.

I worked with Alma Currykosky and Kitty Upholster. When I got bored, Alma gave me a sheet of meat-wrapping paper to draw on, and she always made lunch for me. My greatest fear was going to the bathroom in the basement. The building was old and had dirty walls and a dirt floor. The steps were old and creaky. A single light bulb, suspended from the ceiling, was the only illumination.

Then I went to work at the plant store with Patty Pinto and Connie Gaunt. I mostly dipped cones. By that time, I was in the sixth grade. One day, Connie's boyfriend called and asked for a Big Mac. I was really naïve and didn't know what it was, but I took the order, anyway. Connie told me later that it was just a joke.

When I was in senior high school, I worked at the Ligonier location. It was a really old store, and occasionally a rat appeared from the underground basement that ran under all the stores on the block. We had some very demanding customers there. Once a customer asked for our selection of pastries, and I told her to go next door to Bud's Bakery for them (we only sold donuts).

I hated Fort Ligonier days. I had to dress up in a colonial costume and sell candy. During my teens, I hid and told my friends to tell Dad that they hadn't seen me. I was sure by this time in my life that my future was not with Valley Dairy. I disliked the work itself, but I also resented the fact that I had to work every Saturday morning when all my friends were going skating or having fun. Working was my Dad's rule, but my grandpap had taken him to work at a young age, and Dad was "treating" me to the same discipline. The difference was that Dad liked it.

I remember spending time with my grandpap when I visited him on overnight stays. He took me to the bank to collect rent from his various properties. A handy man always came to the house early in the morning for a meeting. Of course, Grandpap saw to it that I got to work. My grandmother objected to

Three generations of Greubels in earlier family portraits. Left: Joseph F. with granddaughters Mary Jo, Margaret, and Melissa. Right: Joseph F. with son Joseph E. and his wife, Virginia.

this, and would tell him to let me stay at home and help her. Sunday dinners together were always about business, ice cream, or the restaurants. Grandpap certainly was focused on his primary interests.

When I was a teenager, Grandpap took me to dinner and a travelogue - every month. I usually fell asleep during those. Each time he delivered his monthly pep talk - do well in school, be good, help out, etc. etc. The lectures always started with, "Hey, friend!" I knew I was going to hear about some goal in life. He always told me that he never got the opportunity to go to college, even though he had a scholarship. He wanted me to be a doctor, but nursing is the closest I came to that goal.

Grandpap was critical of my boyfriends. I got the "Cow Story" every time I came home with a new one. It went like this: "If you marry a man with one cow, and you have three cows, then you end up with only two cows because you split what you own with your husband. So you should marry a man with more cows than you have in order to move upward in cow ownership."

VIRGINIA GREUBEL, 2004
"I EARNED JF'S RESPECT!"

I first met Joseph F. Greubel when I was a teenager. Even then, I recognized that he was a "force." His personality dominated the local Valley Dairy that I frequented for Cokes and other teenage staples. My memories from that time were of him sitting in a booth, typing the menu for the day.

He always had time to say hello and offer some kind words. He once encouraged my girlfriend to attend a dance and find a nice boy to take her home. He said if she couldn't, he would take her home. Was he surprised when she showed up at the restaurant to accept his offer! And he kept his promise!

As I got to know him later as his daughter-in-law, I learned that there were many more facets to his personality. He was determined, focused, and relentless in business. The first time I saw this in him, I was hurt and embarrassed. I had scoped out a new restaurant in town and reported the findings at the dinner table that night. I was promptly put in my place and sternly advised, "WE go the Valley Dairy!" I came to realize that this was just "Ice Cream Joe" being himself - focused on his business. I always felt that I wasn't liked because I lacked a college education, and I had no professional career.

Over the years, I suppose I did prove my love of the business and the value of my skills. We formed a mutual admiration for each other, or, at least, I was told that he always spoke highly of me.

J.F. and I probably connected more easily on a personal level than a business one. He loved the stock market, and I learned it from him. He loved to buy a stock when it was down and watch it rise, but he never fell in love with any. He always said, "You never go broke taking a profit."

DAVID MCCRACKEN. 2003
"A LOT OF LAUGHTER AT THE VALLEY DAIRY"

Joe Greubel often related to me how he got started with his first store in Latrobe. He went to see his baker to borrow some start-up money. I don't know how much that was. The only thing the banker asked him was, "Well, Joe, if I lend you the money, how do you plan to pay me back?"

Joe answered, "Well, I believe I can make a cone for two-and-a-half cents and sell it for five."

The banker said, "I see you have thought this through," and loaned him the money.

Joe Greubel knew how to make a buck, but I remember seeing in the Ligonier Street store basement several three-wheeled bicycles with boxes on them for holding ice cream. They never made it in hilly Latrobe. Joe bought them cheap in Ohio, but there they lay, unused, a bad investment.

When I told Joe I was going to the seminary to become a preacher, he offered to join me and "take up" the offerings. The Greubels were Roman Catholic, so I often kidded him about having so many Presbyterians working for him. He was the only Gentile in a Jewish investment group in Greensburg, Pennsylvania.

There was a lot of laughter at the Valley Dairy. Joe understood the value of taking care of his customers, and visiting with them. He always jumped in to help his workers, whether it was clearing tables, dipping ice cream, cutting lunch meat, or scrubbing a floor.

When Arnold Palmer won his first green jacket at the Masters, Joe went and asked Arnie if he could use his name on a sundae. Arnold said it was fine. So, Joe added a golf tee to the top of a regular sundae and put a marshmallow on top. He also created the "Pig's Dinner," a banana split in a small wooden trough. You got to keep the trough after you ate the contents.

Joe F. at the counter with employees at the first Valley Dairy store, 313 Main Street, Latrobe, Pennsylvania, ca. 1940s. Nick Waggle is on the far right.

RAY SHEETS, PLANT MANAGER
2004 INTERVIEW
"WHAT ARE THOSE LADIES SITTING THERE FOR?"

Ice Cream Joe would meet me somewhere, and we would ride off to some promotion or other. When we got to a place, he would get out of the car holding a hanger with his Ice Cream Joe vest on it and say, "Hold on. I have to get my luggage." His "luggage" was an old paper bag that contained his hat and ice cream dipper. That just showed me how simple you could make things be, and yet be effective working with the public.

A Youthful Ray Sheets

Once we did a dairy promotion with the Dairy Association in Dubois, Pennsylvania, where we made giant sundaes in a plastic swimming pool. All the farmers were there, together with the reigning Dairy Princess. It was pretty intense, making those sundaes. We couldn't take a break for lunch. We didn't worry about eating. We figured we could eat later.

In Butler one time we were dipping ice cream at a promotion. Ice Cream Joe told the ladies, "Stick around, or come back at closing. We're going to play Post Office." Everybody laughed. Closing time came around. Out on a park bench, near the store entrance, sat five or six ladies. Joe asked, "What are those ladies sitting there for?"

I answered, "Well, Mr. Greubel, you told them we were going to play Post Office after we closed, and that they should stick around."

"They are not!" he said

"Oh, yes they are. They want to play post office. I'm sure of it. You asked them."

I walked out and asked them, "Are you ladies waiting for something?"

"Yeah. We're waiting to play Post Office with Ice Cream Joe."

So I went back and told him, "Yep. That's what they're waiting for."

"We're gonna have to get out of here," he said.

So we sneaked out the back door and made a run for it. That cut down on Post Office invitations.

Joe would go anywhere there might be a potential customer. If I suggested a place, and he could get there, he would make the time. That was his way, that was his business. He loved the public, and he loved the little kids. He'd ask the kids, "Do you know what the one-legged man said when someone asked him how things were going?" Of course, the kids would always answer, "No." Then Joe would say, "Hey, I can't kick!" Then he would have to explain the joke to the kids if they didn't understand it. He loved to joke with them.

Joe F. enjoyed riding in Paul Bell's antique "woody" in the Latrobe Fourth of July Parades.

Ice Cream Joe: THE VALLEY DAIRY STORY

He was big on riding in parades. People would yell, "Hey, Ice Cream Joe!" We pushed that Ice Cream Joe cart down the street, and he would ride in an antique car. He really liked the Willy's jeep we had one time.

Whenever I stopped at his house, Joe would make coffee. Then, we'd sit down and talk about business or his family, past and present. He was very proud of both, especially his sons and grandchildren. They were going to continue the business and carry on his name. He was proud that he was a self-made man, and that he had worked hard for everything he got in life. I heard stories of him going into the restaurants, washing dishes when things were busy. Whatever needed to be done, he would do. When I knew him, he never barked out orders. At least, not that I ever saw.

TOM GREUBEL, 2003
"HE WAS A VISIONARY AS WELL AS A DOER"

I began to work for Joe in 1941, when I was fourteen. I began as a dishwasher, and later worked behind the counter. During the school year, I worked weekends, then full time when school was out. Joe was at the Main Street store in Latrobe, his first store, many hours a day, every day.

Every Saturday night, after closing the store, we hand-mopped the floor, finishing about one o'clock in the morning. Joe paid me twenty-five cents an hour, probably with no deductions. I rode the bus to work from Derry, but Joe usually drove me home because the buses stopped running around eleven at night. Joe didn't show up a few times, so I walked the five miles home in the dark. He caught hell from the parents about that. At the time he was active in the Latrobe Elks — no more need be said.

It was early in war. We had air raid wardens and air raid drills. When the air-raid siren sounded, we had "black-outs." Everybody was supposed to extinguish all their lights and cover their windows so enemy bomber pilots would not be able to find a target so easily. During the ten or fifteen minutes of darkness, I helped myself to some sugarcoated donuts. To me the air raids were a chance to do no work. They were also a chance to get something good to eat.

During the war, we made box lunches for the draftees who were on their way to the train station. In the boxes were a sandwich, an apple and potato chips. I think Valley Dairy got paid $2.00 a box.

Joe made ice cream in the back of the store under conditions that would not pass health inspection today, but to the best of my knowledge, no one complained of food poisoning.

Joe always worked for as long as it took. He was very generous with his time, but much less so with his money. He actively encouraged me to become a physician, and I will always be grateful for this. He pointed out the virtues of being a physician. A physician, he told me, gave service to the community, felt great personal satisfaction, made an above-average income, but at the cost of long and inconvenient hours and family disruption.

Joe always paid for whatever he ate at the store, except for coffee, which he drank in copious amounts. Even when our dad came into the store, he had to pay for everything. When I asked Joe why, Joe answered, "To set an example for the employees."

Early in his career, Joe set a goal to achieve a net personal wealth of $100,000. That figure, he believed, would mean that he was financially successful. At five cents an ice cream cone, that was a distant goal. He read books about stores, restaurants, merchandising, ice cream, and books on how to achieve wealth. One of his favorite books, which was well worn when he gave it to me was Napoleon Hill's *Think and Grow Rich*. Now my son has the book. The pages are brown and their corners are bent, but its message is as current today as it ever was.

Joe was a visionary as well as a doer. Joe once wanted to form an independent bank. Had he done so, he would have been very successful. He was ahead of his time with his Ice Cream Joe vending trucks and the concept of franchising.

Joe did not waste money. He respected the value of money. One time he said, "Once you spend it, it's gone, and you can never get it back." I passed that advice on to my children. When he was asked why he didn't enjoy himself by taking vacations he said, "I'm already enjoying myself. I don't need a vacation." In other words, he was doing exactly what he wanted to be doing.

He never bought a brand-new car until 1987. When his old cars wore out, he went to the auto auction and replaced them. Any color would do, as long as the price was right. In 1987, he succumbed to family pressure and bought a new Lincoln Town Car. He kept it garaged, while he drove his old Cadillac!

When I was in Medical School in Chicago, Joe was there with his right-hand man Roy Moersch. I took them to a strip show in Calumet City, Indiana. My anatomy professor told me that strip shows were good places to see live anatomy in action. All three of us agreed that he was absolutely correct!

After I finished Medical School and moved to California, Joe and I were on a more-equal footing. We were now both adults, even though he was fifteen years older than I was. Our telephone conversations were frequent, and whenever I visited Pennsylvania, he always had a day planned for us to be together. He always appeared in a bow tie, his trademark of dress.

In 1991, I was with my family on a houseboat on Lake Powell. There was no communication with the outside world. When we returned home, I discovered that Joe had died and was already buried. I will always remember him as a brother, a friend, a mentor, a visionary, and someone to be admired.

JANET HUDSON
LIGONIER VALLEY LIBRARY

WORKING AT VALLEY DAIRY IN 1972

My job at Valley Dairy was my first "real" job. Real, in the sense that I received a regular paycheck and had to file an annual tax return. My previous "paying" jobs were limited to Friday night babysitting, walking the neighbor's dog and watering houseplants for people on vacation.

I would like to say that I went to work because I wanted to better my life, plan for the future and learn how to manage my finances. Unfortunately that was not the case.

I was eighteen years old and in the last semester of my senior year in high school. I desperately needed money to buy clothes for college. A college wardrobe was a serious thing in those days. It could make or break the social standing of a student, especially a female college freshman. Coordinated sweaters and plaid skirts were the norm, and a different outfit for every day of the week was mandatory. No one wore blue jeans, sweatshirts or Reeboks except to go hiking or to gym class.

My parents were disinclined to shell out wads of cash for my fashion necessities, so I was forced to find an after-school job. I read the classifieds and saw an ad announcing the opening of a new Valley Dairy store in the Eastgate Shopping Plaza in Greensburg. I loved their ice cream so I thought this would be an ideal job for me.

My older sister and I went for interviews. They were hiring for all positions including deli clerks, waitresses and short order cooks. Deli clerks made a whopping $1.35 an hour. As an added enticement, the deli clerks were also in charge of selling ice cream. I was disappointed to discover, however, that the job benefits did not include all the free ice cream that I could eat!

I was hired on the spot and was secretly delighted that my sister was not. She was in graduate school at the time and her school schedule conflicted with the work schedule. It wouldn't have been "cool" to have an older sister working at the same place and peering over my shoulder.

Before I could begin, I had to purchase a white dress uniform with matching white oxford shoes. Ugh! Those uniforms were hideous and unflattering, especially to a fashion conscious teenager. Besides, they got dirty right away. One little bump with the ice cream scoop and you were suddenly a walking Jackson Pollock canvas. I had to wash and iron my uniform every night after work. Much to my mother's surprise, my laundry skills greatly improved during my stint at Valley Dairy.

My first "non-training" day at Valley Dairy was frantic. It was the grand opening of the store and all of the employees, including the manager, were brand new. People lined up outside the store for the ninety-nine cent chipped ham and ice cream specials. Joe Greubel and his father, "Ice Cream" Joe, dressed in gay nineties striped vests and straw hats, greeted the customers as walked through the doors.

I never realized that there was a right way and a wrong way to make an ice cream cone. At Valley Dairy we made the largest ice cream cones I had ever seen (or tasted). We actually "weighed" the amount of ice cream on a scale. Even though the cone was piled high and ice cream was falling off the sides, we would add more if the weight was not correct. Everyone loved those cones.

We scooped sunflower seed, cherry cheesecake, chocolate peanut butter cup (my favorite) peach, banana split, and mint chocolate chip. New flavors were being introduced all of the time but the old favorites of vanilla, chocolate and strawberry did a steady business. Rainbow was a big seller, especially to the younger children. I was surprised to learn that it is just vanilla ice cream in a Technicolor disguise.

Scooping ice cream turned out to be hard work. By the end of the summer, my right biceps were well-developed and rock solid. I quit wearing sleeveless blouses because my arms looked lop-sided. The ice-cold freezers kept the ice cream very hard and it took a lot of physical effort to make those huge cones. I would cringe when a customer asked for a gallon of hand-packed ice cream. Hand packing a pint or quart was bad enough but a gallon of ice cream required extreme effort. I would scoop and pack and tamp down and scoop again and repeat the process until there was an unbelievable amount of ice cream stuffed into that gallon container. I had to weigh the filled container before giving it to the customer. If the container didn't weigh enough, it was back to scooping, pressing, pushing and forcing in even more ice cream. The customer certainly got their money's worth. I was very happy when we started selling pre-packed gallons in our dairy case.

My favorite job was slicing the deli meat for customers. My father never let me use his power tools because he thought that I would cut off my fingers. The meat slicers at Valley Dairy were large, wicked looking contraptions and fun to operate. I am happy to say that I never had any accidents while using them although I did have a tendency to be a bit dramatic while attempting to slice the more pricey roast beef or pastrami paper-thin. Cleaning the slicers was not as much fun, especially if someone wanted a pound of luncheon meat five minutes before closing.

Operating the cash register was a little scary at first. The register had to balance every night and I was lousy at math. But once I learned to correctly count back change, running the cash register became the easiest part of my job.

For the most part, my co-workers at Valley Dairy were around my age and had similar backgrounds. Friendships, some brief, some long lasting, were formed while working there. It was a great place for my first "real" job.

BILL DYMOND WTRA
(NOW WCNF) RADIO (LATROBE, PA), 2003
"WE HAD A BALL!"

Joe Senior sort of let us do radio promotions exactly as we wanted to. Ice Cream Joe was quite a promoter. He dressed up in costumes and appeared at the stores and in parades. The promotion I recall the most was called "Chapeaus for Everybody" at Torrance State Hospital. We asked people to donate hats to Valley Dairy. At the end of the promotion, we donated the hats to the hospital.

People brought in hats that were 100-years old. At the end of the promotion, the older hats were donated to museums. The rest were given to the hospital. The hat promotion generated almost fifteen hundred hats. It was a huge success, and was covered by all the newspapers. Joe F. and his son saw to that.

Winners of the promotion contests would receive a gift certificate to Valley Dairy, but what I remember most about these promos is the making of them. I had a dawn to dusk station. In other words, we could only operate during daylight hours. In April, we would sign off at sunset, but as the season wore on, the days got longer, and we stayed on the air longer. We had to make the commercials after the station signed off. We worked in the daytime, went home for dinner, then came back and cut the commercials at night. It was all sort of spontaneous. We would write the commercials on the spot, then put them together with sound effects or whatever we could muster up. We had a ball.

All of this was back in 1962. Radio was different then. I doubt whether some of the promotions we did would make it on today's radio.

BOB WILLIAMS, EMPLOYEE, 2004
"THE MAIN THING IS
TO GET THE CASH!"

In 1941, I was working in a golf drive-in near the Latrobe Airport [Arnold Palmer Regional Airport]. We never closed until two or three in the morning. My last two customers every night were a gentleman named Joe Greubel and Bill Blair. Joe always came in wearing an apron stained many colors with ice cream. He told me he ran the Valley Dairy in Latrobe, and would I like to work for him after the drive-in closed for the winter. I told him I was still in school. He told me I could work a shift from seven to eleven at night on weekdays, and maybe an eight-hour shift each weekend day. I took the job at twenty-cents an hour. Those were the good old days!

"Get the cash. The Main thing is to get the cash!" he would joke. What he meant was that the ice cream business was small sales, all cents and nickels. Another time, at a meeting, Joe says, "Now, when I come in and open the cash register, and it's empty, but the merchandise is gone, that's bad, very bad. If the shelves are empty, and there's plenty of cash in the register, that's very good. If the shelves are full, and there's some cash in the register, that's OK, too!" What he meant was that he didn't like the thought of both cash register and shelves being empty. One of them, at least, had to have something there.

Back then, when we closed, we just took the moneybag with the receipts, walked across the street to the police station, and gave it to a police officer. The station was our safety deposit box.

On nice summer days, Joe parked his Chevy at the

back of the store, walk in the back entrance, go up to the front of the store and say, "Get that door open!" He knew what he was talking about. The front entrance was level with the sidewalk. He wanted the door open so that passersby would see the ice cream and ongoing business and be tempted to come in.

On long, winter days I took my homework to the store and got a lot of it done. When I graduated, the war was just winding down, and the Westinghouse plant was still doing pretty well. I left Valley Dairy and went to work at Westinghouse. After a year there, I went back to Valley Dairy. Soon after that, Joe bought a nice plant in Windber, Pennsylvania. His friend, Roy Moersch, ran the plant. I went up there with Roy. This happened just before they started the Ice Cream Joe routes.

I couldn't stand cottage cheese, so I worked on the delivery truck. Joe then sent me down to service the three Latrobe stores. Then Joe opened the Ligonier store, and he promised to put me in charge of it. We remodeled a barber shop. Then we had a grand opening. I had a good friend next to that store. He owned three businesses. We gave his workers free coffee, and that filled up the place. While they were there, they bought our main product — ice cream.

EVE ALBENSI, 2003
"I WANT MORE SALES!"

Joe moved us around a lot in the fifties.

He used to come into the store and check on me once in a while. Sometimes he would be in a nice mood, laughing, and other times he would pound his fist on the table. "I want more sales!"

I used to open up at eleven o'clock in the morning. Joe told me, "Now, before you go inside, make sure you sweep the steps and make the front look clean. If you don't make the front clean, you won't get any customers."

I learned a lot working at Valley Dairy. I met all kinds of people — rich people, middle-class people, poor people. The kids picked up their newspaper bundles and then delivered them in the neighborhoods. A barber in town would come in for lunch everyday. As soon as he got in the door he said, "Give me the ketchup bottle." He put ketchup in his soup, he put ketchup on everything he ate.

MARY AGNES MCGINNIS, 2003
"HE ALWAYS HAD A MUG IN HIS HAND"

My mother, Margaret, was Joe Senior's younger sister. They were very close, and when Joe started school, my mother got so upset and raised such a fuss that the family allowed her to go to school with him. So off they went to grade school and high school. They graduated from Derry Township high school in 1931.

We saw an awful lot of Uncle Joe. He was very outgoing. We always teased him about what a big coffee drinker he was. He always had a mug in his hand.

He was a hard worker, but then he seemed to enjoy people, too. Once, in 1983, when I was in the hospital, he came to visit. We got to talking about people, and he said, "You know, Mary, I have never met a person I didn't like, but I will admit to something. I like some people better than others!" We always got a kick out of that. It seemed so much like Joe. I really don't think he ever did meet a person he didn't like.

NICK WAGGLE, EMPLOYEE, 2003
"THE CLOCK WAS FIVE MINUTES FAST"

I started with Valley Dairy in 1943, at the Ligonier Street store. Later, I made ice cream. It came in fluid form in ten-gallon cans, which yielded about twenty-gallons of ice cream. It was a lot of fun. The girls used to come in and watch me make it. I actually met my wife there.

One day, Joe asked me if I had an uncle named Steve. I told him that I did. This was around Christmas time. Steve was dressed as Santa Claus and had gotten into a car accident. I think he had been too filled with the Christmas "spirit." At any rate, Joe's kids were outside sitting in the car, and little Joe was worried about whether Santa had gotten injured.

Joe set the clock in the Ligonier store five minutes fast, so that people would think they still had time for an ice cream!

TOM HIMLER, 2003
"AM I GOING TO PAY FOR THIS?"

Joe F. always said, "Rent is not important, cost of construction is not important, it's the location!" The elder Joe was a real student of that concept. He was an original, and always pushed for local retail business. He was very concerned when they had a Valley Dairy store in big malls, stores that were becoming less and less popular. He was a real advocate of the freestanding store. Joe was focused on what he was doing, and we made astute decisions. Once in a while he would voice his concerns to me, and they were always business related.

Joe F. was also a funny guy. Back in the late seventies or early eighties, he and I drove to Harrisburg. The Pennsylvania Department of Revenue had some questions about how Valley Dairy was collecting sales tax, what methods of accounting they were using and so forth. Nothing serious. As we drove east along the Turnpike, Joe kept asking, "Are you on the clock? Are you on the clock? I'm paying for this, ya know. All you're doing is driving the car down to Harrisburg, but am I going to pay for this?"

Most people didn't think Joe F. was very generous, but he was. He never asked for any kind of accolade or acknowledgement. He did things anonymously. At holiday time, he had a special interest in people who had no funds. He always made sure they got a food basket. He never wanted anybody to know that he was helping families in financial difficulty.

His son, Joe E., carries on the business with his wife, Virginia, and his daughters Mary Jo and Melissa. Joe F. taught Joe E. well. Young Joe is very good with the girls. He brought them up in the business, and they are very astute business people. He's as much a promoter as his father was, and as frugal. Mary Jo and Melissa affectionately referred to him as "Cheap Joe." If they talked about should they buy this or that for the stores, the two girls would say, "Well, if it's going to be up to Cheap Joe, we are going to get the cheapest (Joe would say 'most economical') one that we can find.

JOSEPH E. GREUBEL, 2003-2004
MEMORIES

Dad was born in Swissvale, just outside of Pittsburgh, but he lived his entire life on First Avenue in Derry, Pennsylvania. He married my mother, Veronica Connolly, who lived at 312 First Avenue, then just moved into the Connolly house. I lived my first thirty-four years there, at what I call the "Connolly-Greubel Hotel." It was a nice, quiet place to grow up in. At 312 I had five "parents" — my mother and dad, Uncle Ed Connolly, and Aunts Agnes and Margaret Connolly. By today's standards, it was a very different sort of life.

With all of us being in the same business it could get a little confusing. My great grand pap was Joseph, my grand pap was Joseph. Their middle initials were both A's, so that made Grandpap Greubel Junior. My dad was Joseph F. for Fleming, after his mother's maiden name. Joseph E. or Joseph Edward, so there were times when I was Joe Greubel III, then I was either Young Joe or Little Joe. One day, when I was about fifty, I was talking to Attorney Tom Himler, and I told his secretary that it was Young Joe Greubel. He got on the phone and said, "Joe, don't you think it's a little pretentious of you, now that your fifty, to keep calling yourself 'Young Joe Greubel?'" After that I didn't call myself Young Joe Greubel any more.

Dad was a graduate of Derry High School. He wrote an essay on chickens and agriculture that won for him a partial scholarship to Penn State University. But Grandpa Greubel told Dad that he couldn't afford to send him. He never got to use the scholarship. Dad took some correspondence courses and a few courses at Saint Vincent College to better himself. One day, my Aunt Agnes Connolly, who worked in the office at one of the mines, called him to tell him that the company was hiring people. He got all slicked up in his white shirt and zipped down there. The foreman took one look at him and said, "We're looking for someone to work on the coal tipple. You look like you're dressed for the office." Dad didn't care. He started that day, the only man on the coal tipple wearing a white shirt.

One day, Dad was paid ten dollars to find out why the Kefer ice cream store in Latrobe was losing money. He found out why. The Kefers said, "Well, if you're so smart, why don't you buy the place?" Dad's response was that he didn't have any money. They responded, "We didn't ask you if you had any money. We just asked you if you wanted to buy the place." Dad popped out with a figure like twenty-five-hundred dollars, though he had only five hundred in the bank. They told him that the offer would be fine, and to go home and get the money. That did it for Dad. The rest became history.

Getting the cash from home was out of the question, so Dad went down to the First National Bank in Derry and saw a man named Fred Kunz, to whom he made a request for a loan. Fred took my dad at his word alone, and gave him what he needed.

Ice Cream Joe: THE VALLEY DAIRY STORY

When he first started, Dad didn't have a car, so he rode the train back and forth from Derry to Latrobe. When he couldn't do that, he slept in one of the booths at the store.

Starting and founding a business for my Dad was really something special. It was sort of like having another child in the family; you want that child to grow, you want that child to do well, and you, yourself, want to be successful. And that's pretty much how my Dad operated. I think what Dad cultivated was a good work ethic. He was a big believer in speedy service. Mother wasn`t in the public spotlight, but they both worked hard for the business and us. My dad used to say, "You never have a better security blanket than your parents." Most people remember my Dad always working in the business, and my mother being at home.

Dad always said, in different situations, "Whatever makes you happy." I'd say to him, "Dad why don't you make a trip to Germany. I know you'd like to go over and visit some of our distant cousins over there, and you'd have a great time. Maybe you'd like to go out to California and visit Uncle Tom?" Well, for one reason or another he wouldn't go, or couldn't go. He would answer, "Well, whatever makes you happy, and I'm happy with what I'm doing."

I started to work with Dad when I was six-years-old. I did easy stuff, at first — washed dishes, put glass bottles back in their cases, stuff like that. I quickly learned that if I hurried up and got things done he would say, "Do you want to go the movies?" There were three movie houses on Main Street, and because we spent a great deal of time at work, I was able to take in three movies a day.

Our days were long. We often stayed until midnight. Mom would say, "You can't take that kid and keep him out all day and night!"

In 1947, when I was ten, Dad promised to take me on a plane ride to New Jersey to get his first Ice Cream Joe truck. Unfortunately, we couldn't make connections, so we ended up taking the train. I liked that. It was one of those overnight Pullmans.

We picked up the truck. It had a canvas roof and a side curtain on the driver's side, and no door on the passenger's side. It had a toolbox, which was all the passenger had to sit on. It was October, and on the way back it turned bitter cold. We were afraid of getting frostbitten, so we stopped in Carlisle. After we got settled in, I said to Dad, "Let's go to the movies!"

When I was twelve, Dad developed the idea of franchising Ice Cream Joe to dealers in areas of Western Pennsylvania, West Virginia, and Eastern Ohio. In 1949, Dad came up with the idea of taking the trucks to Florida, rather than garaging them over the winter in Pennsylvania. Dad had two drivers from the Windber plant drive two trucks down to Florida. Now came my chance to fly in a plane.

One-year-old Joseph E. Greubel. In five years he would be learning to dip ice cream cones.

Dad made reservations for Orlando. For some reason we had to lay over in Atlanta. Having come from a small town, I was shocked to see that the airport had separate drinking fountains — one for blacks and one for whites. That didn't seem quite right to me.

The airline had given us food vouchers at the Dobb's House restaurant. The doorman was the same man who had played Uncle Remus in Disney's Song of the South. I was perplexed. I thought, "How can a guy be a movie star one day, then, all of a sudden, be a doorman the next?"

We went on from Atlanta to Tampa. In Tampa we couldn't make a bus connection to Orlando. I don't know if he approached this private pilot or if the pilot approached him, but he flew us to Orlando for thirty dollars. It was another thrill of a lifetime for me. We flew in a Beechcraft Bonanza, and the pilot, realizing that I was just a twelve-year-old kid, flew out over the Gulf of Mexico. He gave us a really nice flight.

Ice Cream Joe: THE VALLEY DAIRY STORY

Two generations of "Ice Cream Joes." Left: Joseph F. Greubel with his son, Joseph E.

We were in Orlando for two weeks. During that time, we went door to door trying to introduce the Ice Cream Joe idea to people in the area. Dad let me sleep in one time in two weeks.

The two fellows who drove the trucks down stayed in Orlando for the rest of the winter, trying to sell ice cream. The idea turned out to be a dud. Street vending down there was nothing like it was in Pennsylvania. It was just one of those ideas that didn't work out.

Another idea that didn't work out was my clarinet lessons. I did, however, learn a valuable lesson from Dad. One day I said to him, "I'd like to get a saxophone." Instead of a saxophone, I got something else. Dad found somebody who had a used French clarinet for sale. That became my instrument.

"Here," he said.

"Well, I was looking for a saxophone!"

"It's the same family," he said. "If you learn to play the clarinet, you'll be able to play the saxophone."

So I started lessons at school, but there was a big turnover in teachers, and I became frustrated because I didn't feel like I was progressing. Dad signed me up for private lessons in town. My Uncle Bob, my Dad's brother, who drove an Ice Cream Joe truck, would drop me off at my teacher's house. Bob was himself an accomplished musician and even played for a dance band. Dad probably thought that some of his talent would rub off on me. Bob finally got tired of chauffeuring me around, and, anyway, I didn't feel like I was going anywhere with the music.

I told Dad, "Hey, Dad, I just . . . you know, I want to quit taking clarinet lessons.

"You can't do that!"

"Well, I'm not very good at it. I don't have skills like Uncle Bob."

"OK, but there's only one way you can quit. We'll sell the clarinet, and whatever we lose on it, we'll add to the cost of the music lessons. If you promise to pay that back, you can quit."

I worked that whole spring, but didn't get paid. In August, Dad said, "You don't have your debt fully paid, but I think you've learned your lesson. Don't start things you don't plan to finish. So, next week you can start getting paid."

Ice Cream Joe: THE VALLEY DAIRY STORY

In the early days we had a Silex coffee maker. Dad wanted to change it to a new unit, but he couldn't find the shutoff. So he got a guy named Charley Fagan from a plumbing shop across the alley to come over. He said, "Charlie, you disconnect it and I'll shove it onto the new pipe." All of a sudden, a spark shot into the gas line, the gas pipe caught fire, and flames shot up the back bar. Patrick, a young guy working in the store, suddenly started running for the door. "Patrick, where are you going?" Dad yelled. "Mr. Greubel, I got money in the bank next door!" Anyway, Dad took Charley's jacket and beat out the flames. He did buy Charley a new one.

Right up the street was a drug store called "Central Drug." There was a fella up there who had a crush on one of the girls working at Valley Dairy. We had a jukebox then, and he would come in and play the song "Little Girl." He must have worn out that record. I don't know if they ever got to be a number and got married, but he sure romanced her with that song!

Back in the late fifties and early sixties we made a secondary brand — a half-gallon of ice cream called Bluebell, which sold for about sixty-nine cents. And at one point I was trying to get Paul Glosser who was in charge of Gee Bee stores to carry the flavor. At the time they were into a lot of price promotions. Paul laughed and said to Dad, "Joe, it sounds like a pair of pants!" And, actually, there was a trouser company that sold a brand of pants called Bluebell. There was also another dairy down in Texas called "Bluebell." But Paul only knew about the trousers.

Today, we have a fellow who comes in the Windber Valley Dairy by the name of Nick Penetti, who used to service the vending machines. He would say to me, "Joey, whatever nickels fall on the floor, they're yours." Every now and then he'd pitch a few nickels on the floor. I was always diving under a booth or table to get those nickels. Now, when he comes into the store, I say to him, "So you're the guy who put all those lumps on my head making me hop under the tables for those loose nickels you said were mine!"

MELISSA GREUBEL BLYSTONE, 2004
THE COW STORY

My earliest memories of my grandfather were of going to his office at the Valley Dairy Store (as they were called in those days) on Ligonier Street. I loved to go there because I got to look for money on the floor. They used a coin separator that Grandpap said "spilled the coins." I got to keep any coins I found on the floor that had gotten "spilled." I still wonder if that was really true.

I went fishing with Grandpap a lot. We went to Saint Vincent Lake, Twin Lakes in Greensburg, or Donegal Lake near Ligonier, the most. We even went ice fishing. He always put his own twist on everything. When he bought night crawlers, he bought the biggest he could find and then he cut them in pieces to make them go farther.

I never worked side-by-side with Grandpap in the restaurants. I spent time with him at his house in Derry. We would sit on the back-porch swing, or I would make the "rounds" with him to the bank and his real estate rentals. He always came to my school events. He was a real junk food addict, and Grandma always scolded him for giving my sister and me junk food. We often went for soft ice cream at the drive-up places. He smoked a lot. Pall Mall was his brand, and I remember the big, brown ashtray in the living room that was always full of butts. After many years, he gave up smoking, and I was glad he did.

Mr. and Mrs. Joseph F. Greubel on their 50th wedding anniversary celebration at Latrobe's Mountain View Inn

Any time I visited the office and Grandpap wasn't there, I always left him a note. He always answered them through the mail. I loved getting mail from him.

Grandpap had a program for good grades at school. We were rewarded with a dollar for an A, fifty cents for a B, nothing for a C, and then deductions for D's and E's. I loved getting his checks, but I wasn't the best student in the family. I think my sisters made out better than I did.

Memories from my teenage years are sharper. When I started working as a waitress at Valley Dairy, Grandpap would call and get my work schedule. Then he would come in to the restaurant and want to eat with me. This usually upset the manager, because staff were not permitted to sit with the guests.

Grandpap would often call me and arrange a "date." We would go out for dinner at the local Elks Club, Valley Dairy, or other restaurants. This was never very popular with my boyfriends. They couldn't understand why I had to have dinner with my grandfather. At those dinners, I would receive his pearls for living and success. He would say, "Don't paint yourself up with that blue stuff. That's not attractive." He would tell the famous "Cow Story" that all of us got. He would start. "If you have three cows, and you marry a guy with one cow, then you end up with only two cows. But if you have three cows and marry a guy with five cows, then you end up with four cows." He was pretty critical of all boyfriends, not in a mean way. He usually mixed his criticism with humor.

I went with Grandpap to public appearances and charity events. I rode with him in all the parades.

The thing we had most in common was money. I loved making and saving money, and he did, too. I had a paper route, baby sat, worked in a local pie shop, and then at Valley Dairy. He saved pennies in huge jars that he hid in his bedroom. He showed me where they were, and he trusted me to keep the secret.

My early training included our annual coupon-clipping party, when he brought his bonds to the kitchen table where we clipped the coupons for a whole year, put them into months, and got them ready to take to the bank when they were due. I was fascinated with this ritual, not so much with the worth of the coupons, but with the maturity dates that seemed a lifetime away. The ritual always included going out to dinner. I still have the note he included with my first share of stock.

Unfortunately, I never had the opportunity to learn more about that kind of investing.

In his later years, Grandpap took to spending part of the winter in Florida with his brother. One year, he got pneumonia and was hospitalized. That was the first time that I realized he was getting old. He always seemed young to me.

After Grandpap passed away, I moved into his house in Derry. I lived there until I graduated from college (which he didn't get to see. I know it would have given him great pleasure). Then I went to work full-time with Valley Dairy.

SUMMER, 1998
FROM IN AND AROUND LATROBE
LATROBE'S ENTREPRENEURS...

Joe F. Greubel offered new, tasty menus featuring luncheon and dinner specialties. In fact, Valley Dairy advertised seven delicious plate lunches every day. Many old time customers remember watching Joe sitting at a booth in the rear of the store with his portable typewriter making up the menu for the next day. He made an original and four carbon copies for the waitresses.

One of Joe's first signs, which hung in the store for decades reflected his personal creed: "QUICK FRIENDLY SERVICE, CORRECT PROPORTIONS, SENSIBLE PRICES."

Although he initiated new dairy store items and products, ice cream, hand-made nightly in the back of the store, was the key. Joe offered thirty flavors and he was famous for his "skyscraper" cones, tall scoops that sold for a nickel. On a typical Saturday night, in the booming 1940s, the employees and Joe would scoop over 1,000 cones.

Joe's second store was on the corner of Minahan Avenue and Ligonier Street next to the Latrobe High School. His third store was on Lloyd Avenue in the 6th Ward.

One of Joe's early workers was Guy "Buzz" Yolton, whose father was the town burgess. Guy wrote an early newspaper ad for Joe that became a framed slogan on the walls of Valley Dairy stores: "Wind, rain, snow and sleet, Valley Dairy plate lunches are always a treat!" That slogan was influenced by Buzz's role as Head Cheerleader for the Latrobe High School "Wildcats."

Another Valley Dairy success was the marriage of James Visconti and his wife Sylvia, who met while working at the Valley Dairy. Today, it's Dr. James

Visconti, a chiropractor. Sue Pohland also worked in the Latrobe store and had a happy homemaking career as the wife of the Penn State football coach, Joe Paterno.

One of the many tales about working at Valley Dairy is that of a young worker who came to Joe and announced that he was planning to get married in a week. Joe, who was working at his tiny desk in the corner of the kitchen looked up and said, "When is the wedding?" The young man stammered and answered that the ceremony was set for 10:30 a.m. on Saturday. "Good," said Joe, "You can work until ten, go to the church and get married, and then hurry back here for the noon lunch trade. After that, you can go on your honeymoon." And that's exactly what Jim and Louise did.

Another longtime employee was the late Bill Rakotis. One day, Joe was walking down Main Street when he saw Bill getting a haircut. Later, when Bill was back at work, Joe chastised him, "I don't think it's good business for you to get your hair cut on company time!" Unperturbed, Bill looked at his boss and said, "Gee, Mr. Greubel, my hair grows on company time."

It wasn't long before Joe's stores were packing in downtown merchants and professional people for lunch. Joe reserved a round table for Dr. Bob Steele (a dentist), insurance man Bill Woods, and Dr. John Braillier (a dentist and son of the first professional football player), Leon Klingensmith, Chevrolet dealer Theron "Ted" Smith, and Fred Graham, a denture maker. Sam Aronson, a grocer, always brought his own Kosher bacon when he wanted a BLT.

Harry Hostetler, a Dodge dealer, brought his salesmen after closing for a milkshake. He urged them to look at the friendly and anxious-to-please clerks. "Men," he would say, "I am inspired by the great attitude of the Valley Dairy staff. This is how I want you to greet our customers."

One night, in 1959, the original store closed at quitting time, and the entire store contents, freezers, ovens, broilers, counters, booths, tables and cash register, got moved one block west to a new location. Joe E. Greubel remembers how everyone pitched in with trucks, dollies and carts. The new store opened the next morning for breakfast.

AUGUST 15, 2003
FROM DON A. "CAM" DOMINIC
1951 LATROBE HIGH SCHOOL FOOTBALL TEAM
"AND A TREAT IT WAS"

How sweet those memories are, even today, some fifty years after tasting Ice Cream Joe's delicious Valley Dairy sundaes and milkshakes. You see, even then, Joe Greubel know how to effectively promote his product. What he did was offer a free ice cream product to every Latrobe football player, win or lose, at his downtown Latrobe store. The store was located near the old Olympic theatre, and after each game all of the guys would walk from the high school to enjoy their treat. And a treat it was! After those rough and tough games the store would be filled with fans wanting to talk to the players about this or that touchdown and what would be in store for the next opponent. I recall sitting in one of the chairs that lined the wall, eating my sundae, and chatting with my classmates and townspeople. We had a lot to talk about in 1950, because that group of Wildcats went 9–1. We came in second in the Western Pennsylvania Interscholastic Athletic League. I never had a chance to talk to young Joe Greubel, but if I did I would want to thank him for what his father did for the football jocks of that era. It was a beautiful way to thank the local athletes, and, at the same time, generate enthusiasm and loyalty between the school and the town.

I'm a long way from home now, but my roots are still back there with the team and the sweet memories about delicious ice cream treats from Ice Cream Joe Greubel.

2004
A FINAL WORD
FROM JOE E. GREUBEL

One time I was in the driving an Ice Cream Joe truck down a back road. I didn't have all the experience in the world. The gas pedal pad fell off and the little metal rod got stuck on the floor. The engine was running wide open. If I had been smart enough I would have just turned the key off. I rode the truck down full throttle, stomping at the floor and picking at the rod with my foot trying to get it to come back out of the hole in the floorboard. I got down to the dip in the bottom of the road. I started up the hill, when the knob popped out. I probably wasn't the only one to have that experience. We put a lot of miles on those trucks, day in and day out. Anyway, I was young, and it was some kind of experience for me!

Back in 1951 and 1952, when I was fifteen, one of

my jobs was to go along as sidekick on all the Ice Cream Joe trucks so that I would learn all of the routes, and be able to break in new drivers. By the time I was sixteen and able to drive, I could take a route if someone needed a day off. With all the use we gave those trucks, there were times when things weren't up to snuff, like slipping emergency brakes and things like that. One day I working down in the Jeannette/Grapeville area and I was going up a long, steep street. Some guy in a bathrobe opened his front door and started to wave at me. He wanted some ice cream. I knew it was going to be hard to stop on that hill. I stopped and got the emergency brake on and it seemed to be holding pretty well. I eased my way out of the door to come around the side door where the products were. I hollered at him to see what he wanted. He yelled back that he wanted ice cream sandwiches. Carefully, opened the side door. I knew if I wasn't careful, the truck might drift backward. I walked from the road up the walk to the house, and I'm standing on the porch giving the guy his ice cream sandwiches, and he's in the process of paying me. Suddenly, his mouth opened wide and his eyes got big. I though "uh-oh," and I turned around and looked and there was the truck inching itself a foot or so at a time back down the hill. I made a hasty retreat to the truck, got in, hit the brakes, and got that problem solved. After that, I hoped I wouldn't have to make any sales on steep hills.

The first year I took complete charge of the plant was 1964, and it was a brutal year for me. That year was training year for the boss's son. Luckily, I had help from my brother John, and Angeline Horner It was the year that someone broke in, cracked the safe, and handed us a major loss. I got so upset about the burglary that I rolled the safe out of the front of the building and pitched it over an embankment. I thought that any passerby would see it and realize that we no longer had a safe to rob.

Then a young guy working on the pop crew took one of the delivery trucks out for a joy ride. He didn't have a driver's license. He overturned the truck on someone's lawn, laying out a whole load of Popsicles.

We had trucks that were equipped with ammonia hoses hooked up to the refrigeration system that ran off the plant. Then a serviceman forgot about the hookup, and pulled a truck out. The heavy-duty rubber hose didn't break, but the fixed pipe in the wall did, and the ammonia went through the whole building. It was so bad that the green guests checks turned pink.

That year I had disgruntled employee who went to our biggest customer and proceeded to tell him how dumb I was, and what a nincompoop I was, and how incompetent I was. Luckily, that customer was smart enough to continue to do business with us and not to take a disgruntled employee's word that I was that bad. I really wasn't. I was just going through some very tough experiences, and getting some I probably wouldn't have gotten otherwise.

In the early days, My dad could always be seen sitting in a booth at one of the stores with *Wentzel's Menu Maker*, a giant book, ten or twelve inches thick. It looked like it was the "World Encyclopedia of Everything." He would sit there with that book and a standard typewriter, pecking out menus. He never forgot "fruit Jell-O salad" or "beans and franks." He had another popular item — thin, wafer cuts of steak, quickly cooked, and served on a bun with lettuce and tomato or whatever. Back then milk came in glass containers, and the cream sort of floated to the top. Sometimes the milk had like a bluish tint to it, but this was corrected after homogenization came into play.

There were a lot of things Valley Dairy did that were probably ahead of their time. We were one of the first to produce diabetic ice cream, a sugar free product. We actually had ice cream companies selling those products. I worked with Rose's Dairy down in Connellsville going out on their trucks and visiting their accounts. At the time our flavors were limited. We had vanilla, of course. Coffee was a flavor we could produce because we could use the instant flavoring without sugar. We had a chocolate that was sugar free. The vanilla and a coffee were very good and quite natural flavors, but the chocolate didn't quite have the same color to it that regular chocolate ice cream has.

Back in the 1950s we had a product called "Plenty Pleasing." It was an ice milk product, and low calorie. Back then, low cal wasn't the thing it is today, so "Plenty Pleasing" had only a marginal success. Just a few years ago we worked on a project with Pfizer Pharmaceutical to produce a fat-free product. That, too, had minimal success. Basically, people are more interested in real ice cream that has fat content and flavoring. Most people are smart enough to know that it is best to eat a little less.

In the 1950s, there was a company in Cincinnati called G.P. Gunlach Company. They were very big on creativity and came up with unusual names for flavors. They used to hold an annual seminar, some of which I attended with Dad. Mr. Gunlach always said, "Give someone a sample of ice cream in a spoon. When they have the spoon in their mouth ask them how they like it. They will shake their heads yes, because if they shake them no, the spoons will fly out."

That was one of his Gundlach's tricks of the trade. He was one of the creators of the White House flavor. He also had Bavarian Strawberry, and some unusual twists on Carmel flavors. Gundlach's gave you a little handbook and point of sale signs. They were a real quality flavoring house back then, and one of the few people in the flavoring business that had point of sale or signs available to go with their flavors if you bought their flavoring.

There was a guy in town who was one of Dad's competitors. He later became a Borden's distributor. During the war, he was on the Rationing Board. Somehow, he managed to limit or stop Dad's sugar ration. Of course, that meant that Dad couldn't make enough ice cream to survive, if, that is, he could make any ice cream at all. I don't remember how, but Dad did manage to find a source of sugar, so that broke up the guy's attempt to put Valley Dairy out of business.

Then the guy got to be a member of the local Draft Board. He set his sights on getting Dad drafted. That didn't work either. What Dad did was get a job as a night watchman at a factory that made casings for machine-gun bullets. So, he worked the store in the day, and went to his night watchman job at night. Because the factory was classified as a defense installation, Dad got a deferment as a defense worker.

I think his competitor finally gave up on the matter.

There were lots of funny things that happened over the years. Lots of sad things, especially people leaving. When you work with someone for many years, you think you will have them forever. But you don't. They retire. You still have the good memories, though, and that helps make up for things.

A 1960 Valley Dairy employee party at Monroeville, Pennsylvania's, Holiday House. Right side, front to rear: Mary McManamy, Dorothy Uncapher, Kitty Upholster, Virginia Mullen, John Landa, George Harr, John Greubel, Dick Myers.

Left side, rear to front: Nell Beck, John Levendosky, Helen Spewock, Joe E. Greubel, Virginia Kabala Greubel, Lil Lear, Eve Albensi.

JOE F AND THE FAMILY GREUBEL... OVER THE YEARS AND ROOTS

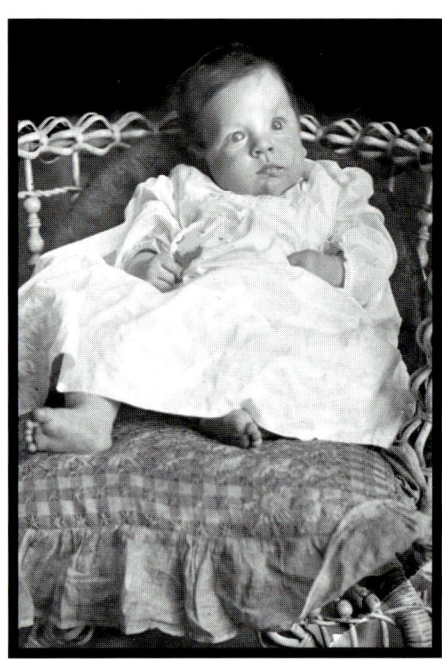

Left: Joe F. Greubel's baby photo.

Center: Edna Fleming Greubel holding her children, Joe F. and Margaret, in 1915 or 1916.

Bottom: Joe F. and Nick Rich in their work clothes, and an unidentified friend on the right taking a break behind Ziegler's Bakery in Derry Pennsylvania.

Left: Roy Moersch, Steve Marcinko, and Joe F. Greubel in New York City, 1940s. Moersch was Joe F's partner during the Ice Cream Joe franchise years.

Center: Joe F. in 1946. He proudly poses in the Valley Dairy corporate office on Latrobe's Main Street, the corporate seal next to his right arm.

Bottom: Joe F. attends to promotional materials at the Ebensburg, Pennsylvania, Valley Dairy (1972).

Ice Cream Joe: THE VALLEY DAIRY STORY

Joe F's parents and grandparents.
Standing left to right: John Greubel and Joseph A. Greubel, Jr.
Seated left to right: Joseph A. Greubel, Sr., George Greubel, Mary Greubel, William Greubel, Carolina Ziegler Greubel.

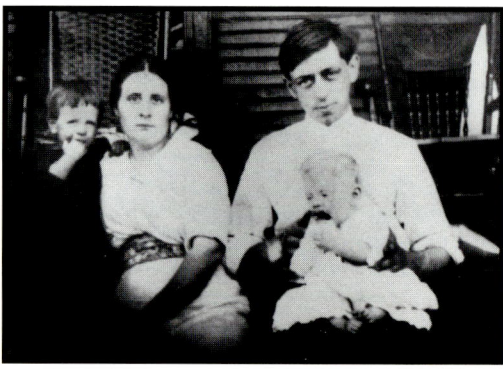

Top: Joseph F. Greubel (left), mother Edna and father Joseph A. Greubel, Jr., holding baby Margaret.

Center: Joe F's father Joe A., who was the Assistant Postmaster in Derry, Pennsylvania.

Bottom: The Greubel siblings, with cousin Clem.

Ice Cream Joe: THE VALLEY DAIRY STORY

Joe F. and his family. Wife Veronica, Joe E. (left) and brother John.

Joe E. with wife, Virginia, Mary Jo Sell (left) and Melissa Blystone at the corporate headquarters, Latrobe, Pennsylvania. Spread out on the table are blueprints for a new Valley Dairy.

Ice Cream Joe: THE VALLEY DAIRY STORY

"GREUBELISMS"

JOSEPH F. GREUBEL

"It's best to grow old with money. At least someone will pay a little attention to you."

"Germans will go through a brick wall before they will look for a door."

"Our business reputation far exceeds our bank account."

"If you could start out old and get younger, everything would get better."

"I don't know a lot about religion, but I do think people are better off with than without."

"If you can't save a penny, you won't save a dollar."

"You can't do business with an empty wagon."

"Make few promises, but keep all that you do make."

"Try always to do more than you promise."

"Anybody can captain a ship when the seas are calm."

"In business, when everybody is happy, look out!"

"When someone throws you a negative, put a stroke through it for a positive, and keep going."

"I never met a person I didn't like, but there are some people I like better than others."

"Never poke around in a rattle snake's nest. Let it bite someone else."

JOSEPH E. GREUBEL

"You'll never have a better security blanket than your parents."

"Travel when you are young. The memories will last longer."

"Don't try to outsmart your parents. They have already been there."

"Treat each day as a blessing and a bonus."

"If you must kill time, try working it to death."

"Business has no comfort zone. You can't coast."

"Everytime you quit making an ice cream flavor, it was at least one person's favorite."

"In a family business, you never get the job you are most qualified for, but rather the one that was most recently vacated."

Pittsburgh Press, "Roto Magazine," ca. late 1940s – early 1950s

THE LEGENDARY ICE CREAM JOE... BEGINNINGS, FRANCHISES AND PROMOS

DECEMBER 1950 *Dairy and Ice Cream Field*

ICE CREAM JOE OF LEGENDARY FAME BRINGS ADDED PROMINENCE TO AREA

Ice Cream Joe, the colorful and legendary character created by the Fairview Dairy, Inc., with headquarters in Latrobe, has grown from a toddling youngster to a full-blown giant of the ice cream industry within a period of a few short years.

Born in 1946 of the fertile minds of two Latrobe men, Joseph Greubel (President) and Roy Moersch (Secretary/Treasurer), this symbol of a boy whose hat is crowned with ice cream and whose body is encased in a cake cup is known to thousands of Pennsylvanians in more than twenty communities.

Ice Cream Joe is also a national institution, for on April 11, 1950, his creators received a national copyright and trademark registration in the name of "Ice Cream Joe."

Few persons have traveled as extensively as this popular lad, for he is seen daily on a huge fleet of Ice Cream Joe vending trucks operated by Fairview Dairy and twenty-one franchise dealers throughout Western Pennsylvania, Ohio, and West Virginia. This Herculean feat is made possible through a system of Ice Cream Joe franchises that have been authorized by the owners of Fairview Dairy.

According to these working agreements, people in other communities throughout three states are legally privileged to use the Ice Cream Joe trademark on ice cream containers, advertising and vending equipment that are provided for their use by Fairview Dairy. Each licensee is given a protected territory in which to operate.

Ice Cream Joe vending trucks are white with standard designs that include striped awnings, loudspeakers for music, and abundant lighting. The vehicles are to be seen daily in residential areas,

> "Television is something that is troubling movie houses, bars, night clubs, even soda fountains, because people with television sets stay home more than they used to do. We don't worry about it, because we take our ice cream right to the home,"
>
> *- Joseph F. Greubel*

school locations, and are eagerly awaited by scores of patrons of all ages.

The fascinating character of Ice Cream Joe, considered a working subsidiary of the parent concern, employs his extensive talents in a number of ways.

Not only is he seen on all wrappers and containers of ice cream products sold by Valley Dairy stores and all franchise dealers, but also many of the products have assumed his name — Jo-Sandwich, Jo-Cups, Jo-Pops, and Jo-Drums.

Ice Cream Joe's popularity has been enhanced because of his generosity to the small fry to whom he gives valuable prizes in exchange for wrappers and lids from Ice Cream Joe products. Lids from half-gallon containers have a value of twenty-five points, lids from pint containers, eight points, wrappers from Jo-Pops, one point.

The prizes are also point-rated, and they come in a wide variety — toy fire trucks, musical batons, love birds in gilded cages, ukuleles, gold ball-point pens, flashlight guns.

Because of the prize program, the volume of mail Ice Cream Joe receives each day rivals that of many Hollywood stars, and often threatens to overflow the office located in the Commercial Bank Building. Two clerks devote all of their time in replying. They also mail the prizes.

Although Ice Cream Joe enjoys a more extensive popularity among his smaller patrons, grown-ups also benefit. Motorists, especially, have become aware of him, because during several days of the pre-Christmas season, he checks the parking meters several times a day, and, when he discovers a violation, he inserts coins to extend the parking time. Joe then wishes the motorist a Merry Christmas and Happy New Year by placing a card on the windshield.

DAIRY AND ICE CREAM FIELD, OCTOBER 1949
"ICE CREAM JOE"

Roy Moersch and Joseph Greubel, officers of Fairview Dairy (Windber, PA), were seeking a simple design to identify their first street vending truck. They felt it was necessary to pick a simple name for a character that would be easily recognized and remembered.

Their originality led to the "birth" of "Ice Cream Joe." Their "baby" received such great public acclaim that additional ice cream trucks were soon necessary to meet the popular demand of the citizens of west-central Pennsylvania for Valley Dairy ice cream, and it was just a question of time before it was decided to utilize this magnetic personality for the firm's merchandising and advertising programs.

A great deal of credit for the public's widespread acquaintance with Ice Cream Joe must be assigned to the fact that he travels extensively by truck in his neighborhood. Valley Dairy has five vending trucks and a scooter, all of which are on the streets seven days each week during the season that begins in the middle of April and ends in October. The vehicles cover heavy residential areas, school locations, and other established routes. A typical truck will cover an assigned route on alternate days, and the working day for the commission-basis drivers begins at 11 a.m. and concludes at 11 p.m.

Ice Cream Joe: THE VALLEY DAIRY STORY

Below: One of the ads Joe Greubel created to attract franchise dealers to the Ice Cream Joe franchise. Right: Copy of the notice Valley Dairy personnel placed on the windshields of cars.

VIOLATION

Was showing on your parking meter. I took the liberty of putting in 2¢ to extend your parking time.

Signed _____

Ice Cream Joe

P.S.—Merry Christmas and A Happy New Year

VALLEY DAIRY STORES
Latrobe . . . . Ligonier

DON'T READ THIS!

Unless YOU ARE A PROGRESSIVE, FINANCIALLY RESPONSIBLE ICE CREAM MANUFACTURER INTERESTED IN VOLUME SALES WITH GREATER PROFIT IN 1951 AND YEARS TO COME.

If you meet these requirements . . . if you have the fortitude and foresight to proceed with a proved profit-making merchandising program aimed at selling ice cream directly to homes in your territory . . . then you are ready for progress with an . . .

ICE CREAM JOE *Franchise*

For complete details, write, phone or wire

ICE CREAM JOE
Commercial Bank Building   Latrobe, Pennsylvania

Reprinted from the December, 1950, issue of The Ice Cream REVIEW.

'Howdy Folks! Ice Cream is my business. I am ready to serve you every other day at your home, office, special event, factory, starting today. I'll be up and down your street with your ice cream treat in my new refrigerator cooled truck! You'll save steps, and I'll have what you want in my new ice cream truck! Listen for my musical horn. Watch for me.'"

— *Ice Cream Joe Handbill*

These trucks are something to see, and plenty Pennsylvanians see them. Accessories on each unit include striped awnings, lighting, musical horns and chimes that sound a "Merrily We Roll Along" theme, and others. This progressive ice cream firm has found truck vending to be an integral part of its overall program.

Ice Cream Joe is present in all of the firm's [five] retail stores. The company first made use of him on point-of-sale signs in the stores to promote weekly fountain specials like ice cream sundaes selling at prices slightly under regular prices — hot-fudge sundaes at 19 cents (regularly 25 cents), for example.

A weekly column appears in the local papers under the signature of Ice Cream Joe. The column is composed of local news and incidents of interest to children. It is written in language children find easy to understand. Mention is made of members of the "Kiddies Club" who are ill, members' birthdays, new members, letters from members and similar items. The youngsters are encouraged to write Ice Cream Joe, giving him "dope" for his column.

To complement this phase of the Valley Dairy ice cream promotion program, get well and birthday cards are sent at appropriate times to members. In addition, a free birthday sundae is offered to every member of the club at "Happy Birthday" time.

Ice Cream Joe: THE VALLEY DAIRY STORY

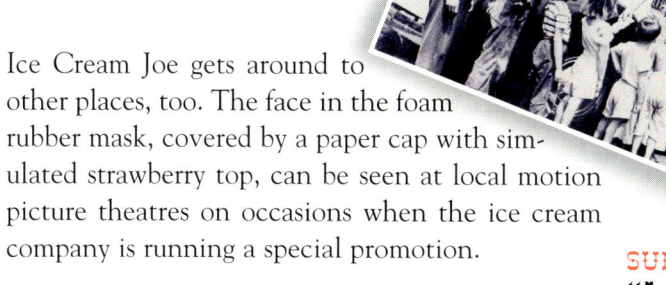

Ice Cream Joe gets around to other places, too. The face in the foam rubber mask, covered by a paper cap with simulated strawberry top, can be seen at local motion picture theatres on occasions when the ice cream company is running a special promotion.

Such is the popularity of Ice Cream Joe that his employers have found it expedient to copyright his name and character. From the standpoint of expansion and future operations with their pet achievement, the firm's executives, Messrs. Moersch, Greubel, and attorney John S. Lightcap, Jr., have announced that they are in the process of setting up franchise Ice Cream Joe operations in different localities.

SUMMER 2003
"I WAS AN ICE CREAM JOE"
- Bill Hughes

"Those white trucks had all those ribbons and bells. Ice Cream Joe driving around, ringing the bells, all the kids coming out. I was sixteen in 1951-1952. I could go in and out. I wasn't restricted to mileage. I'd work half days, and I would be done. We were very busy, very popular. The guys working inside stocked the trucks and counted the stuff. When I got back, I had to come with the money or the ice cream, so there was a system of checks and balances. You could get a Cheerio for a nickel, an ice cream cone, or a Jo-Pop. Everything was a nickel, basically. Everything sold pretty well. Since we catered mostly to children, the nickel stuff sold the best. It wasn't very expensive, and

The kids line up for ice cream and premiums.

Ice Cream Joe: THE VALLEY DAIRY STORY

One dealer in Gallipolis, Ohio, couldn't afford a motorized vehicle. Joe Greubel was perfectly amenable to the dealer using a horse and buggy.

most kids could scrounge a nickel somewhere. Back then, I was an Ice Cream Joe, and I still love ice cream. Valley Dairy still has the best vanilla ice cream in the country."

AUTUMN 2003
"JOE PAID FOR THE GAS"
- David McCracken

I worked for Joe Greubel and Valley Dairy Stores off and on during my high school, college and post-college days, covering a period of about ten years.

My first encounter with Ice Cream Joe was in the summer of 1951, when I rode along in one of the trucks with my boyhood friend, Dale Henry (now a retired Marine). We were servicing the Ligonier route out in the Rolling Rock Farms area off Route 711. Most of our sales were small nickel items—Jo-Pops, ice cream bars and ice cream sandwiches. So, when we had the opportunity to sell pints and half-gallons of ice cream (for $1.20), we'd go for it. We only made 15% of our sales, but Joe paid for the gas. Dale knew a farmer who always bought a half-gallon, so away we went down a country road. On the way, we had to ford a small creek. It was a hot, humid day, so we stopped mid-stream, took off our shoes and began to wash down the truck. Suddenly, a horn blew behind us.
We turned, and there was Joe Greubel himself. He'd been following us.

"What do you think you're doing? he asked. Then he turned around and left.

I've done a lot in my sixty-eight years, but the hardest job I ever had was being Ice Cream Joe in the summer of 1952. We usually loaded the truck by nine o'clock in the morning behind the store on Ligonier Street in Latrobe. I often drove the Blairsville Route and stopped at all the little coal towns between Derry and Blairsville. When I went up and down the streets in Brenizer, with all those jingles like "Mary Had a Little Lamb" playing, I'm sure every mom and dad hated to hear me coming. I sometimes hated to hear me coming! We had to be careful, for often little kids would run out in front of us, and the older boys would try to steal ice cream from the rear door.

When we did stop, it seemed that every kid in the coal "patch" would surround the truck. The major item I sold was five-cent Jo-Pops. I averaged 700 Jo-Pops a day. If you do the math, that comes to $35.00. I got $5.25 for that.

The kids would all shout at once. "What kind do you have?" So, I would shout back, "Orange, cherry, banana and grape."

"Don't you have root beer?"
"No."
"Would you repeat what you do have?"

Now, you would think that in a group of ten or fifteen kids at least one would remember the flavors I just rattled off to the last customer. But no one ever did. They were too excited to pay attention. Finally, after the thirteen biggest kids made the largest purchase of their lives, the two smallest, with dirty faces and hands, looked up to me and said "Ice Cream Joe." One would hold out his hand, holding only a penny, while often the other would hold out an empty palm. "Here, kid, have one on me." So, usually I made $5.15.

When we did the premiums, I had a real job sending out the toys that the kids saved their sticky, dirty Jo-Pop bags for. If you think I ever totally counted all those bags, you'd better think again. Most of the kids printed what they wanted and where they wanted their gift sent. Several times, however, I got requests with no return address. Usually, if I waited a few weeks, I would get a follow-up letter. Once, one said, "Hey Joe, where the hell's my firetruck?"

Those summers as Ice Cream Joe, I practically lived on ice cream. I also knew when the manufacturing plants took their breaks. We could snoop out a Jo-Pops sale within a mile, and a half-gallon sale within five miles.

One night, I returned home and found my parents watching Jackie Gleason and the "Honeymooners." That night Ralph Cramden came home from work as a Good Humor Man. Audrey Meadows, playing Alice, said, "Sit down Ralph, and I'll fix you a nice ice cream sandwich." As Ralph washed up, Alice said, "Hurry up, Ralph, your sandwich is getting warm."

I suppose that was an inside joke for ice cream vendors.

Chester A. College, Latrobe Chief of Police (1952-1954), seen here with members of the Ice Cream Joe Kiddies' Club. Chief College helped form the Latrobe branch of the Kiddies' Club. Each year he would organize bus trips for the kids to the Pennsylvania State Police Rodeo in Pittsburgh's South Park. Local merchants helped with food tokens and other expenses. The buses departed from the Valley Dairy store on Latrobe's Main Street.

"ICE CREAM JOE"

Don't want no Baskin Robbins.
Don't want no Haagen Daas.
Don't want no Frujen Glas.
Don't care how much it cost.

Don't want no Ben and Jerry's.
Don't want no Tom Carvelle.
Don't want no Breyer's Natural.
Oh, can't you hear the bell?

Here he comes ... Ice Cream Joe!

Don't want no Steve's Original.
Don't want no Dreyer's Grand.
Not even trips to D.Q.
Will give me what he can.

Give me a Nutty Buddy.
Give me a Sno-Cone please.
Give me an ice cream sandwich.
That's all I really need.

Hot summer day,
With all my friends at play
Hopin' that his truck will pass our way.
Give me a quarter please.
This fall I'll rake the leaves.
I'll promise anything for
Ice Cream Joe.

Here he comes ... Ice Cream Joe!

Hey, Joe!

[A song by a young man who remembers his boyhood. Ned Regan wrote the lyrics for his Ice Cream Joe song in 1989. John Michaud, Frank Genovese and Chris Klym wrote the music. Their group, "Cigarette," recorded the song under the Pensongs label].

Ice Cream Joe: THE VALLEY DAIRY STORY

Top left and bottom: Ice Cream Joe trademark applications, approvals, and renewals. Top right: A 1950 invoice signed by Roy Moersch on behalf of the Ice Cream Joe Company for the purchase of five Dodge trucks, designed according to specifications.

Ice Cream Joe: THE VALLEY DAIRY STORY

THE SCHNABEL STORY

The Schnabel Company, builders of all types of refrigerated and insulated truck bodies, has the experience of 91 years of "know how" to offer the Dairy Industry. Whether it's an Ice Cream Vending Body, or a large route truck of over 1500 gallons capacity, Schnabel is the manufacturer from whom you'll want to buy. Schnabel bodies are in operation with Sealtest, Meadow Gold, Borden's, Foremost, Abbotts, Bowman, and a long list of other prominent dairies, besides a host of smaller users, operating in forty states and seventeen foreign countries.

If your needs are large or small, retail or wholesale milk, or an ice cream body, call, write, or wire

THE SCHNABEL COMPANY
Pittsburgh 3, Pa.   Established 1860   HUbbard 1-3000

A brochure created by Fairview Dairy and the Schnabel Company. Insert: The Ice Cream Joe/Schnabel truck on display at a National Dairy Show. The truck was supposed to serve as an inducement to other ice cream vendors to purchase Ice Cream Joe franchises, or perhaps create franchises of their own.

YOUR "DOOR OPENER" TO VOLUME SALES AND GREATER PROFITS

A PROVED, MERCHANDISING, PROFIT-MAKING PROGRAM

Research reveals that in one week's time, an average family of four persons, plus a minimum allowance for a few guests, consumes at home, several quarts of ice cream. That amounts to hundreds of quarts a year per family. Which proves beyond a doubt that *Today's Biggest Market for Ice Cream is the American Home.*

In five months, *two million nine hundred twenty-seven thousand* packages of ice cream bearing the "ICE CREAM JOE" label, were sold directly to homes in Western Pennsylvania by "ICE CREAM JOE" dealers. That's selling it the "ICE CREAM JOE" way.

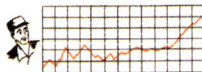

One of our dealers who never sold ice cream before, and operating only one "ICE CREAM JOE" unit, sold more than $1,200.00 worth of ice cream in one week. That's an average of over $170.00 each day. And with our guarantee of a 40% gross profit, this man is really making money. You can too, with the "ICE CREAM JOE" program.

The "ICE CREAM JOE" truck plays an important part in opening the doors of this tremendous *home market.* "ICE CREAM JOE" bodies are built by the SCHNABEL COMPANY, a Pittsburgh, Pennsylvania concern with more than 90 years' experience in fine body building. They are mounted on sturdy, new DODGE job-rated chassis. No wonder customers welcome "ICE CREAM JOE" dealers in their neighborhood with these colorful, sparkling, spick-and-span trucks.

Without question, "ICE CREAM JOE" is the Ice Cream Industry's fastest growing merchandising character. In less than a year, twenty-one franchise dealers have been established in Western Pennsylvania alone, and all of them are showing excellent returns and making money.

Exclusive territories are open to financially responsible persons. A nominal cash investment is required.

For an appointment with our representative
Write... 'Phone or Wire:

"ICE CREAM JOE"
Fairview Dairy, Inc.
Commercial National Bank Building
LATROBE, PENNSYLVANIA

Ice Cream Joe
"ICE CREAM JOE" REG. U.S. PAT. OFF.   DISTRIBUTOR FOR
THE SCHNABEL COMPANY • DAIRY INDUSTRY TRUCK BODIES
South Tenth Street   Pittsburgh 3, Pa.   HUbbard 1-3000

FAIRVIEW DAIRY INC.

Top: Kids pose with their treats with the very first Ice Cream Joe Truck. Inserts: An Ice Cream Joe truck showing the original colors; one of Ice Cream Joe's ads with the Greubel catch phrase, "Howdy Folks!" Below: A row of Ice Cream Joe franchise trucks. John McKool, franchise dealer, is on the right.

Ice Cream Joe: THE VALLEY DAIRY STORY

Ice Cream Joe franchise dealers and their trucks. Center: Ezzard Charles, world heavyweight boxing champ, enjoys the ice cream cone he bought from Ice Cream Joe franchise dealer Mike Namey of New Kensington, Pennsylvania. Bottom: Art Weiskircher, of the Ohio Valley Dairy Products Company, East Liverpool and Martin's Ferry, Ohio, with an Ice Cream Joe fleet.

Ice Cream Joe: THE VALLEY DAIRY STORY

Top: The Griffins, of Butler, Pennsylvania, with their franchise truck.

Center: Ice Cream Joe driver in New Kensington, Pennsylvania, seated on a variant of an Ice Cream Joe vehicle.

Center left: An Ice Cream Joe franchise promo card.

Bottom: An early milk truck based in Windber, and used for home and store delivery.

Ice Cream Joe: THE VALLEY DAIRY STORY

*Bill Rakotis
Joe Greubel
Looking over a few
of the requests for
Ice Cream Joe Premiums
August 1950*

> Top: Joe Greubel and Bill Rakotis fill orders for premiums at their office in the Mellon Bank Building, Latrobe, Pennsylvania. Bottom left: Ice Cream Joe exhorts the local boy scouts. Bottom right: Joe Greubel (left) and Roy Moersch greet Ice Cream Joe in front of the Ligonier Valley Dairy (1946). The Toyad Company of Latrobe made the character's head. Saint Vincent College provided a pair of trousers from a band uniform.

THE PREMIUMS AND PROMOS

Ice Cream Joe: THE VALLEY DAIRY STORY

The Ice Cream Joe premium list featured prizes for kids who saved the wrappers from various ice cream treats. Charles Kaylor, Sr. of Kaylor Displays in Greensburg, Pennsylvania, did the drawings.

Custom Made Bags of Long Island, New York, made Ice Cream Joe's "Jo-Pop" bags. Ice Cream Joe sold more than one million Jo-Pops in 1952.

Top and Bottom: I scream, you scream, we all scream for ice cream! Grand opening of the Valley Dairy store in Latrobe, Pennsylvania's, Sixth Ward was a wonderful treat for children in the mid-1940s. Joe Greubel poses with an oversized "Ice Cream Joe" head, surrounded by a group of children. These scenes in front of the Lloyd Avenue store were used in a slide presentation "Sixth Ward Memories" presented by attorney Ned J. Nakles, Sr. and the Latrobe Historical Society on September 5, 1996 at the Latrobe Elementary School. Courtesy of the Latrobe Area Historical Society.

Ice Cream Joe: THE VALLEY DAIRY STORY

THE HOWDY DOODY CONNECTION

In Western Pennsylvania, West Virginia and Eastern Ohio, the Ice Cream Joe character became so popular that only Santa Claus rivaled him. By August 1952, Ice Cream Joe was receiving more than 30,000 pieces of fan mail and premium requests each month. Ice Cream Joe's fame was receiving national attention, and requests to become an Ice Cream Joe dealer were coming from all over the country. There were so many that it became difficult for the Greubel to follow up on all the leads. Moreover, Ice Cream Joe had national purchasing contracts with Dodge trucks, Sealright Packaging, and other major suppliers. The notoriety attracted the attention of the Doughnut Corporation of America, owner of the popular character, Howdy Doody. DCA, wishing to develop its own line of ice cream novelties and to help market the Howdy Doody TV show, set out to acquire the Ice Cream Joe dealer network. Joe Greubel and Roy Moersch were amenable to the idea, since their concept had grown beyond their financial and physical capabilities. As part of the sales contract, Roy Moersch was given a position with DCA, and Joe Greubel turned his attention Valley Dairy stores, which had been somewhat neglected during the Ice Cream Joe years. In 1954, DCA, through a contract technicality, stopped payments, and the Ice Cream Joe trademark was returned to the Greubels. DCA, at any rate, got what it wanted — a dealer network and a key person in Roy Moersch. Roy continued to work for DCA until his retirement.

The nationally-known Clarabelle the Clown from the Howdy Doody Show in Latrobe (1953), as a guest of Valley Dairy. Here, Clarabelle greets young fans at the Old Athletic Field on Ligonier Street. No one seemed to mind the rainy day.

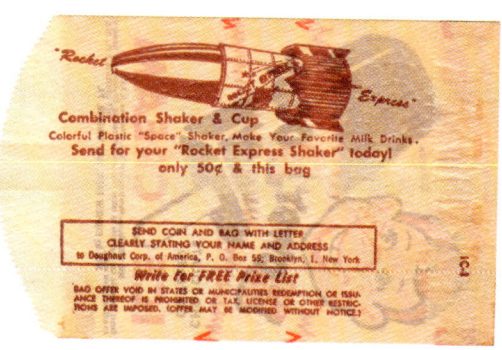

Ice Cream Joe: THE VALLEY DAIRY STORY

THE SALESMAN

[This piece on the universal Salesman was a source of encouragement to Ice Cream Joe.

The source was Charles A. Kaiser and Associates, Cleveland, Ohio]

And in those days, behold, there came through the gates of the city a salesman from afar off, and it came to pass as the day went by he sold plenty.

And in that city were they who were the order takers and they who spend their days in adding to the alibi sheets. Mightily were they astonished. They said one to the other, "What the hell; how doth he getteth away with it?"

And it came to pass that many were gathered in the back office and a soothsayer came among them. And he was one wise guy. And they spoke and questioned him saying, "How is it that this stranger has accomplished the impossible?"

Whereupon the soothsayer made answer: "He of whom you speak is one hustler. He ariseth very early in the morning and goeth forth full of pep. He complaineth not, neither doth he know despair. He is arrayed in purple and fine linen, while ye go forth with pants unpressed. While ye gather here and say one to the other, 'Verily, this is a terrible day to work,' he is already abroad. And when the eleventh hour cometh, he needeth no alibis. He knoweth his line, and they that would stave him off, they give him orders. Men say unto him 'Nay' when he cometh in, yet, when he goeth, he hath their names on the line that is dotted."

"He taketh with him the two angels, 'Inspiration' and 'Perspiration,' and he worketh to beat hell. Verily I say unto you, go and do likewise."

TOPPINGS

The ice cream industry in the United States produces more than $20 billion in sales per annum, and the figure is growing. On average, each American eats around six gallons of ice cream a year. The figure assumes that all ice cream that is produced is eaten. more than any other nationality.
[Assumes all ice cream produced is consumed]

In the United States, July is the month when the most ice cream is sold. This fact, however, is probably not the reason President Ronald Reagan declared July "National Ice Cream Month" in 1984.

At any one time, there can be thirty to forty delights available under the brand names Popsicle, Fudgesicle and Creamsicle.

The Twin Popsicle pop was created during The Great Depression, thus making it possible for two people could share a Popsicle. so two children could share a Popsicle ice pop for just a nickel.

Good Humor trucks, including Ice Cream Joe's, sold various kinds of ice cream bars, among which were Vanilla with Chocolate, Chocolate-Chocolate, Toasted Almond, Chocolate Eclair, Chocolate Fudge, Coconut, Banana Split, Fresh Banana, Fresh Strawberry, and Coffee.

JANUARY 1984:
THE ICE CREAM BUSINESS IN BOMBAY, INDIA

According to my research, real American-style ice cream did not make its appearance in India until the mid-1950s. Until that time, the closest thing resembling ice cream was a thing called kulfi, and fruit ices. The plant I visited in Bombay is now freezing ice cream on early model Vogt continuous freezers, and stick confections are made using the brine-tank method. There are several company-controlled outlets, and there are over 1,000 franchised dealers in Bombay and other cities.

Most parlors have open fronts, and keeping them clean is a problem because of dust and dirt. The franchises offer twenty-two bulk flavors, which are packaged in small square-packs of about one gallon capacity. They dip from visual cabinets of their own design and manufacture. A single-dip, three-ounce cone sells for 3 to 4 Rupees (thirty-five to forty-five cents), depending on flavor. Single-dip sundaes are sixty cents; milk shakes (made on ordinary household blenders) are sixty cents. Floats (made with bottled pop) go for seventy-five cents, while banana splits cost one dollar and twenty cents.

Stores also sell novelties and factory-filled packages for "take-away." Sundae toppings include raspberry Melba, lemon, orange, vanilla, strawberry and chocolate. Some of the more interesting ice cream flavors are tangy mangy, coolfi delight, kessar nuts, mango ripple, mint jazz, and fudge fruttie.

More than seventy-five percent of business takes place at night.

By the way, my friends in India think I'm a big shot here in America. Please don't tell them anything different!

DECEMBER 1985:
SODA JERK.... A VANISHING SPECIES

soda jerk, s_'da j_rk, n. [Amer. Slang, becoming obsolete; term derived from the short, sudden pulling motion applied to the soda draft arm in (the operation of) making an ice-cream soda]. One who works at a soda fountain.

Courtesy of Ed Marks

A dictionary definition shouldn't be necessary, but my own scientific survey shows that most people under the age of forty have never heard the term "soda jerk." Shocking! A campaign, like the one environmentalists initiated in the 1970s to "save the planet, must be launched on behalf of that vanishing breed who once routinely dispensed ice cream sodas—and a whole lot more—from behind soda fountains all across America.

The soda jerk—at the peak of his popularity from the late 1800s through the 1930s—was a member of a highly respected profession, sought after by thousands of youthful, red-blooded Americans. Dominating the scene at drug and confectionery soda fountains, these dedicated young men (seldom young women) took on many roles. Apart from the obvious one of making sodas, the soda jerk prescribed remedies for upset stomachs, headaches and hangovers. Pepto Bismol, Bromo Seltzer, and Alka Seltzer were dispensed right at the fountain at a nickel a shot. The soda jerk was casual counselor to countless customers, turning a sympathetic ear to the lovesick youth and administering counter-side advice along with his delectable fountain treats. And, of course, it was he who invented all those great ice cream concoctions we take for granted today. What kind of life would it be without hot-fudge sundaes, double-chocolate sodas, root-beer floats, and banana splits? How soon we forget!

Ice Cream Joe: THE VALLEY DAIRY STORY

Magazine covers courtesy of Ed Marks

JUNE 1987:
SOME PRETTY GOOD DEALS

Innovator, counselor, entertainer! All in all, the soda jerk made America a better, happier place in which to live. We need to preserve this proud part of our American heritage. We need to publicize our cause! Are you listening, friends?

Let's call upon our President to order the printing of a special commemorative SODA JERKS postage stamp. Let's lobby the U.S. Congress to proclaim a "National Soda Jerks Day!" Let out the schools, close the banks, shut down government offices, bring out the fireworks and brass bands. Let's celebrate the national holiday with parades, with dancing in the streets! Do your part to save this time-honored American institution before the term "soda jerk" is lost to history!

Joe Greubel cuts some pretty good deals with the six or eight Pennsylvania radio stations that cover the trading area for his thirteen Valley Dairy Stores. He furnishes them with certificates good for half-gallons, sundaes, and sometimes for dollar amounts redeemable for food and ice cream. Arrangements vary from one station to another. Sometimes it's dollar for dollar at retail in exchange for commercial airtime; other times it might be half trade, half cash. At any rate, he gets plenty of extra plugs for announcer ad-libs. The promos bring certificate winners and their friends into the Valley Dairy stores. Radio stations use certificates for on-the-air giveaways, sales prospecting for new accounts, customer gifts, etc.

Ice Cream Joe: THE VALLEY DAIRY STORY

AUGUST 1987:
SAVE THE ICE CREAM SODA

In 1984, I alerted you to one of the great tragedies of this century—the disappearance of the ice-cream soda from the American scene. I put the blame for this national calamity onto beverage dispensers; operators can lease them for dispensing their carbonated drinks instead of investing in expensive soda fountains.

For years, I have insisted that one cannot make a genuine ice-cream soda without that fine stream of soda water, which is standard on all soda fountains. The sizzling sound of that jet stream gave the soda its authenticity.

But is the final product any different from a soda made with the coarse stream? Yes, somewhat. The finer stream creates smaller bubbles and a foamier head. But does it taste any better?

The melting away of the ice-cream soda has caused me considerable consternation and sleeplessness. I have had to increase my medicine for hypertension. Finally, after a lot of thought and experimentation, this old soda jerk officially (but sadly) decreed that an ice-cream soda could be made without the fine stream of soda water.

AUGUST 1987:
OUR FOREIGN CORRESPONDENT

Joe Greubel was in England recently on a fact-finding mission. "Food prices are higher in London than in the U.S.A," he reported. "A cup of coffee ranges from eighty cents to $1.70." He sent along a menu from the "New England Ice Cream Parlour" located in Harrod's world-famous department store (we borrow names and concepts from the Old Country; they Americanize their menus). A blurb on the Harrod's menu states: "New England ice cream is made with fresh cream from an early-American recipe. The natural ingredients of our ice cream and toppings are the best obtainable anywhere, at any cost. Fountain concoctions at Harrod's are pretty pricey. A two-scoop dish of ice cream is £1.75, standard sundaes are £2.75, double-dip sodas go for £2.20, and a thick milkshake if £2.20. Fancy sundaes with names like "Star-Spangled Banana," "The Boston Coffee Party," carry out the New England theme, and are priced from £2.75 to £3.45. "It takes $1.65 to $1.70 to equal one pound (£)," says Joe, who is now reviewing his own menu to see if he can increase prices!

NOVEMBER 1987:
DID YOU GET CREAMED? YOUNG AND OLD WORKERS FRESH CONES

Did you get creamed in the recent stock market crash? I did. Though I didn't have a lot invested, I had hoped there'd be enough left when I cashed in—for the woman to cash in—to give me a decent memorial service. Now, unless the market recovers, there won't be enough left for the deluxe package and a party afterwards. Upsetting! My first thought was to drive downtown and jump off a tall building like the losers did during the 1929 crash. Then, I happened to remember that our town is so small it doesn't have any tall buildings!

We continue to hear and read a lot about the decreasing labor pool of young food-service workers. It's not getting any better. I still see lots of "Now Accepting Applications" signs at many locations, even big banners across the fronts of buildings. I was in a Burger King the other day where they placed a flyer on every tray. It headlined: "They Laughed

When They Heard I Worked for Burger King." Then it listed the advantages—extra spending money, new responsibilities, new friends, etc.

A lighted Help Wanted All Shifts sign hung above the counter. It listed even more advantages—flexible hours, free uniforms, meal discounts, paid training, competitive starting rates.

At a McDonald's I found three fast-food grannies in back of the counter. They were doing a great job, too! McD's used table tents and tray liners with the theme "All That's Missing Is You" to attract the older worker. Various enticements are listed along with a color photo of a white-haired gentleman about my age in a red McDonald uniform. Youthful co-workers, including a couple of pretty young ladies, surround him. It made me want to rush to my nearest McDonald's and apply, but I realized that our town was too small to have a McDonald's.

Joe F. Greubel in the parking lot at the Windber Hospital for a benefit and TV commercial.

NOVEMBER 1987:
THE DAY I MET JOE F. GREUBEL

I first met Joe F. Greubel, founder of the Valley Dairy chain, about forty years ago at a National Dairy Convention in Atlantic City. He was running around the convention floor sporting a giant "Ice Cream Joe" badge. A "wild and crazy guy," I thought at the time. But the senior Joe's flamboyant talents paid off; he built a profitable business that is still growing. A number if years ago he turned the reins over to his sons and attempted to retire. I say "attempted" because company prez Joe E. Greubel continues to defy the federal labor laws to protect senior citizens by forcing the old fella—along with his antique push cart—back out into the streets.

On October 10, for example, son Joe had his dad don his Ice Cream Joe apron, then ordered him to push his cart over to the big Hess's Department Store in the Johnstown, PA, plaza and give away ice cream samples. Hess's was featuring a "Good Old Days" spectacular, replete with antique displays, giant cake, free balloons, hot dogs, and concerts, among many other things, as a way to celebrate their 90th anniversary. Of course, the ice cream dispensed from an old-fashioned cart fit right in. The event gave folks a chance to meet the Original Ice Cream Joe, who has become somewhat of a local celebrity; it also gave a lot of exposure to Valley Dairy.

On October 15, PM Magazine from WJAC-TV, Johnstown, was hosted from the Valley Dairy store in Richland. Once again, Ice Cream Joe was wrested from his easy chair to make a personal appearance on the program. The next day, the Valley Dairy cart was seen at the Alumni Association booth during the 1987 University of Pittsburgh at Greensburg Fall Festival.

Then, on October 24, the coercive son ordered the senior Greubel to suit up once more and appear with his cart in front of the Valley Dairy at the Dubois, PA, mall. Here he took part in a Jefferson County Dairy Promotion that included a remote-radio broadcast. He was then pressured into assisting the Dairy Princess as she handed out ice cream samples. And that's the way it goes! The younger generation always takes advantage of us oldies because they know we work cheap!

MAY 1989:
THE BLIMP

With the trend toward smaller families and live-alones, the pint-size carton of ice cream has made a comeback. No one is more aware of this than trend-watcher Joe E. Greubel. So when he introduced their new "Parlor Flavor" premium pint in April, he pulled out all the stops.

Naturally, he conned his old daddy, Joe F., into doing some sampling at their mall location. Customers purchasing two pints at the $1.59 sale price were given a free ice cream scoop. "Some customers even got free hugs from Dad," says young Joe. "We had to remind him several times, 'It's free scoops, not free hugs!'"

At Valley Dairy's freestanding unit, a mini-blimp was used for drawing power. The fifteen-foot-long, eight-foot-diameter blimp, tethered with 300 feet of rope, was moved from store to store. Valley Dairy purchased the blimp from a California company. "Later on," says young Joe, we plan to use it at our wholesale accounts and in parades." The blimp is also a traffic stopper. One time State Police had to stop traffic so the blimp could be moved across the highway. Housing the blimp so far has not been a problem. Airport hangars and car washes serve the purpose very well.

JUNE 1989:
ICE CREAM CAKES FOR AIR TIME

You do remember radio, don't you? It's like TV, but without a picture. And it's still an effective medium for a lot of advertisers. Rates are kind of high, though. But this doesn't deter our number-one contributor, Joe E. Greubel, from using radio. His latest wrinkle is trading decorated ice cream cakes for airtime.

To introduce a new line of ice cream cakes to Pennsylvania, Joe worked out a deal with the powerful (50,000 watter), Key-95 WKYE FM/WJAC AM Johnstown, PA, radio station. The only cost to Valley Dairy was one ice cream cake per week. Here is the announcement: "Key 95 and Valley Dairy are going to celebrate. What are we celebrating? Why, your birthday, or your anniversary, or any special occasion you want to celebrate. Let us know of a special event coming up for you, and we will celebrate by giving you a delicious ice cream cake from Valley Dairy." Listeners send in a post card with full information. Each Wednesday, "Big Jim" the morning announcer, announces the weekly winner.

Incidentally, the press continues to follow Valley Dairy's mini-blimp from store to store. Result: many stories and pictures in the press. "Like a kid with a toy balloon," certainly applies to Joe.

OCTOBER 1989:
YOUR HIT PARADE

Well, Joe E. Greubel might have another hit on his hands, one that could turn into a publicity bonanza, and it didn't cost him a dime! Former Johnstown, PA, native Denny (Ned) Regan is associated with a major California recording studio. He also writes and performs songs with a West Coast rock group. Because Ice Cream Joe was a boyhood memory for Denny, it served as an inspiration to compose words and melody for a tune titled (what else?), "Ice Cream Joe." The lyrics are clever: "Don't want no (several nationally known ice cream brands mentioned here). Give me Ice Cream Joe!" As the kids would say, "It has a good beat." Poet Records produced the tape. "They asked for our permission to use the name since it is our copyright," says Joe E. The recording has not been marketed. "They may wait until National Ice Cream Month next year to introduce it. While the song is not yet in the "Top Ten," I believe it has commercial possibilities.

NOVEMBER 1990:
WORK FOR FOOD AND DIAPERS

It was Saturday, October 20, at the Anaheim, California Convention. We had meetings at the Marriott covering almost everything you could think of—procurement, biotechnology, product tampering, solid wastes—you name it—fourteen in all. Virginia Greubel attended the one on employment law. I attended the ice cream/yogurt session. People were walking out because the air conditioning was at the "blizzard" setting.

At lunchtime, the Greubels asked me to ride with them to a unique restaurant they had discovered. The place was called Mimi's Café, a popular local chain. When the check came, I gave Joe a lesson in "outfumbling."

On our way back to our hotel, we saw a young woman standing on the curb at a busy intersection, clutching a small baby, and holding up a hand-lettered sign "I NEED WORK IN EXCHANGE FOR FOOD AND DIAPERS."

As times get tougher, and we see more and more struggling single moms, will signs like this become commonplace?

JULY 1990:
VALLEY DAIRY GETS FREE AIR TIME

Valley Dairy received free airtime when Johnstown's (PA) 50,000-watt WKYE/WJAC radio station held an open house a few weeks ago. Listeners were invited to tour the studios and production facilities and meet station personalities. Following the tour, guests were treated to Valley Dairy's new frozen Yogurt and met the original "Ice Cream Joe" (Joe F. Greubel, company founder), who is a well-known local personality himself. Son, and company Prez, Joe E., has worked closely with broadcasters in the past. Last year he gave away ice cream cakes in weekly drawings held by radio stations.

MARCH 1991:
VALLEY DAIRY AND DESERT STORM

Yellow ribbons have become almost as much of a national symbol as Old Glory itself. Employees at Valley Dairy Ice Cream Parlors and Restaurants started wearing yellow ribbons right at the beginning of the Desert Operation, even before the Shield became the Storm. This is a good example of the way to show support for the young Americans serving in the Mideast.

NOVEMBER 1992:
AWARDS AND GO BANANAS!

Valley Dairy was honored at an awards presentation held at the Pasquerilla Performing Arts Center, University of Pittsburgh, Johnstown Campus, on September 18. The Johnstown Tribune Democrat sponsored a "Simply the Best" competition for the various retail establishments ("Best Men's Clothing," "Best Fun Place to Shop," "Best Happy Hour"). Valley Dairy CEO Joe E. Greubel attended the black tie affair to receive top awards for "Best Ice Cream Shop" and "Best Milkshake."

Speaking of Joe, when he runs an anniversary sale, he believes that a really super value, like "Buy One-Get One Free" will attract the attention of people who perhaps have never been in a Valley Dairy Store. For the company's recent 54th anniversary, Joe promoted two for the price of one special on banana splits, half-gallons of ice cream, and half-gallons of frozen yogurt.

MAY 1993:
JOE E. GREUBEL GOES HISTORICAL

Valley Dairy received accolades and publicity for its part in the Latrobe Area Historical Society's "Sixth Ward Memories" program on March 18 at the Latrobe American Legion Hall. The event, conceived and presented by local attorney Ned Nakles, featured an evening of stories, photographs, exhibits and a slide show of early industries and businesses. A newspaper story included a photograph of the grand opening (1944) of a Valley Dairy store, showing the original Ice Cream Joe surrounded

The Valley Dairy "Summer Hummers," of Johnstown, Pennsylvania, pose with Lindsay Blystone, Joe E. Greubel's granddaughter, at the East Gate Shopping Center in Greensburg, Pennsylvania, a Valley Dairy location. The Hummers were also known as the Knights of Harmony. Valley Dairy used them in many promotions. Left to Right: Walter Hutzel (Hollsopple, Pennsylvania); Jim Seesholtz (Tire Hill, Pennsylvania); Javier Pelayo (New Enterprise, Pennsylvania); Tony Marshall (Everett, Pennsylvania).

by dozens of kids. Joe E. Greubel and secretary-treasurer Virginia Mullen (now in her 54th year with Valley Dairy) furnished ice cream and dipped free cones for attendees. Latrobe, PA, as you may recall is the birthplace of the banana split (1904).

OCTOBER 1993:
THE SUMMER HUMMERS

It's been a while since we mentioned Joe E. Greubel. So that his friends won't think he has expired, we have reproduced a card to prove the old promoter is still promoting. His sale of $1.99 "Good Old Summer Time" Strawberry Banana Splits last June set new records and created a Bull Market in Chiquita stock. A barbershop quartet, "The Summer Hummers," added to the promo.

JANUARY 1995:
SWEETHEARTS

Valley Dairy's "14¢ Sweetheart Sundaes" is an annual promotion, according to Joe E. Greubel. Buy any regular sundae and get the second one for just 14¢. Joe used a clip-on menu and sales persons' ribbons. So, now that you've taken care of Valentine's Day, Joe, what are you going to do for St. Patrick's Day?

SEPTEMBER 1995:
OUR PLACE OR YOURS?

The number one principle of advertising is "getting the message across in as few words as possible." Joe Greubel's 31 Valley Dairy highway billboards do just that. Their message, OUR PLACE, OR YOURS?

Ice Cream Joe: THE VALLEY DAIRY STORY

VALLEY DAIRY FAMILY RESTAURANTS. 13 LOCATIONS, tells the whole story of what Valley Dairy stores are all about—food, fountain, and packaged ice cream. Joe gives credit where credit is due—to his wife Virginia. She came up with the "Our Place or Yours" theme, he admits.

JANUARY 1997:
MORE THAN ANY OTHER "FIZZ-ICIAN"

Joe E. Greubel gets more free publicity than any "fizzician" I know. An example is a greeting card by award winning artist Peg Panasiti of Latrobe, PA, who remembers frequenting a Valley Dairy store as a child. She has titled her watercolor "Soda Jerk." It is rendered in the style of the great French impressionists—Renoir, Degas, Monet, and so on.

JULY 1997:
MASHED POTATOES, GRAVY, AND THE ICE-CREAM IMAGE

How does a mashed potatoes and gravy restaurant—such as the Greubel family's Valley Dairy—serve complete breakfasts, lunches and dinners, and still maintain its ice-cream image? For one thing, they feature a special ice cream dessert, usually a sundae, banana split or parfait at a special price on both lunch and dinner menus. Combination specials are promoted, too. Also, journalists who are always writing about the store's history, people, and its involvement in community affairs often highlight Valley Dairy as an ice cream establishment.

MAY 2000:
NATIONAL ICE CREAM MONTH

National Ice Cream Month evolved from a promotion called "Ice Cream for America." Sponsored by the International Ice Cream Association, it was kicked off on Capitol Hill on June 23, 1983. Over 7,000 senators, representatives, government executives and staffers waded through 2,000 gallons of ice cream, 5,000 novelties, and seventy gallons of toppings. Senator Strom Thurmond was judged "cham-

pion eater" of the afternoon by "consuming more ice cream with more enthusiasm than any other member of Congress present." The event was reported to be the "largest turnout ever for a Congressional reception."

It didn't take long for the politicians to realize they could get free TV face-time when the cameras caught them enjoying America's favorite dairy food with its politically correct, wholesome image. Result? The following year (1984), Congress and President Ronald Reagan designated July as "National Ice Cream Month," and the third Sunday in July as "National Ice Cream Day." President Reagan, by the way, spoke at the combined NICYRA convention in Anaheim, CA, in 1990. "I'm a dessert man myself," he confessed, and recalled when "chocolate and vanilla were the only two flavors available, and now you see tub after tub of flavors."

MAY 2000:
A LITTLE HISTORY AND DILL PICKLE ICE CREAM

The Hyatt Regency Hotel near Chicago's O'Hare Airport held an Ice Cream Hyattfest on Saturday and Sunday, July 23, 1983. I was invited as a guest to judge a sundae-making contest. I had them convinced that I was some kind of celebrity—the last of the great soda jerks! I furnished ten gallons of Dill Pickle ice cream.

Long-time NICYRA members Ben Cohen and Jerry Greenfield were there. The dynamic duo had driven their van full of ice cream all the way from Vermont without a stopover. I was so impressed by their wild enthusiasm I predicted they would become successful and famous, and I told them so. Was I right, or what? Of course, I knew that Ben and Jerry had sold out to Unilever in mid-April for $326 million.
I enjoyed the Lana Turner look-alike contest. She was the movie star discovered working at a soda fountain when she was sixteen. She became known as the "Sweater Girl."

The "Ice Cream Pig-out" attracted sixty-eight-year-old Hymen Polonsky, who was listed in the Guinness Book of Records as the "World's Greatest Ice Cream Eater." But Hymen quickly lost his title (unofficially) to twenty-three-year-old ice cream slurper Ernest Faudel.

JANUARY 2002:
JACKETS FOR CONES

It seems that designers and inventors have been concerned about dripping ice cream cones since the first one made its debut at the 1904 St. Louis World's Fair. Through the decades, dozens of design patents and utility patents have been granted for drip collars, drip holders, even a cone with its own, built-in drip collector.

I came up with a few of the losers and winners.

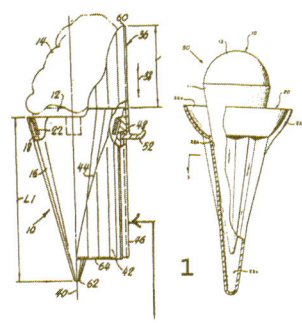

Drawing 1: A guy from Brooklyn applied for a patent in 1988 for the engineering marvel on the left. The one on the right, a 1967 model, hardly needs to worry about drips because of the itty-bitty scoop of ice cream. *Drawing 2*: Robert Sotile, a medical systems expert, may be the first to bring a practical cone holder to market. Bob applied for a patent on his "Buddy System" in 1995, and was awarded the patent in 1997.

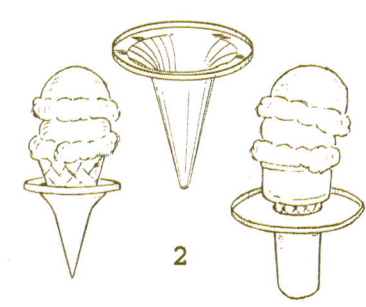

The thin, plastic holders are now available. The advantages to Bob's system are obvious: they catch the drops, there is no contamination from change making, and they impress today's germ conscious consumer as well as health officials. *Drawing 3*:

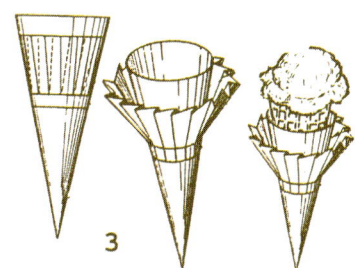

David L. Rodman recently designed this "Tidy Cone." After examining his unique paper jacket/drip-collecting device, I would say he knows as much about the origami paper-folding art as the Japanese do. It comes in one size and fits the sugar cone. Dave thinks it might add three cents to the price of a cone. *Drawing 4*: Joseph Schoenfeld was granted a

Ice Cream Joe: THE VALLEY DAIRY STORY

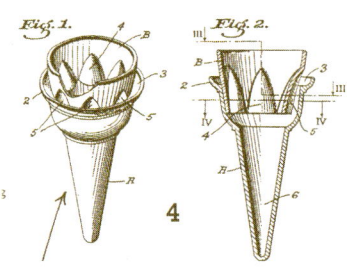

patent for this one in 1933. As a kid he must have dropped the ice cream off his cone, so he probably designed the three-pronged affair to secure the ice cream and, for an encore, circled the cone with a trough for the drips. <u>Drawing 5</u>: Dorothy Boynton applied for a patent on this ruffled drip-catcher in 1929. With her over-dipping, it probably didn't do much for drips. Besides, the bare hand is contaminating the cone with coliform germs. <u>Drawing 6</u>: Back to the drawing board for the 1979 contraption on the left. The 1990 one in the center had its own trough, but didn't go over very well. The 1939 model on the right didn't fly either, but you gotta admit, it has nice, clean, no-nonsense lines!

JULY 2002:
THE BATTLE OF THE TITANS

The contest for media attention continues between Joe Greubel, head honcho of the Valley Dairy chain and Henry Gentry, Jr., owner of Henry's Homemade Ice Cream, Plano, Texas. Seems like I'm always reporting on why the press is attracted to these two promoters—so much so, it's embarrassing. Valley Dairy's latest visit by the press occurred when three gals, and a boy named Justin, all from the Valley News Dispatch, descended on the Franklin Village Mall restaurant for lunch. The newspaper's very next issue featured this headline: "CREAM OF THE CROP." The line underneath in bold print read: "Lunch Bunchers Find Heavenly Desserts at Valley Dairy."

What did Joe do to attract the attention? Nothing. So it had to be the food, the ice cream, and the service. Here are a few comments by the reporters: "Good service and a fine lunch at a neat and tidy restaurant." Justin, the "Junior Lunch Buncher" (it was "Take Your Child to Work Day") proclaimed the cheeseburger to be delicious.

As a matter of policy, the newspaper paid for the meals to confirm the article was "unrelated to advertising."

Valley Dairy scored another photo-op a few weeks ago in Whirl, a highbrow publication on Pittsburgh's social scene. Joe was pictured in his trademark "Ice Cream Joe" getup,

Joseph E. Greubel and Harry Gentry, owner of Henry's Homemade Ice Cream in Plano, Texas, pose for the camera. It is believed that Henry might have won the Best Necktie competition (had there been one).

AUGUST/SEPTEMBER 2002:
BLOOD-LETTING AT HENRY'S AND JOE GREUBEL'S SUNDAE SCHOOL AWARD

Seems like I'm always writing about Henry Gentry, the premier promoter of Plano, Texas. He just won't go away. Neither will Joe Greubel. The "Battle of the Titans" never ends.

"Joe Greubel can't keep up with me," Henry brags. Joe admits, "Keeping up with Henry is tough."

Pajama parties have been popular at ice cream parlors for two decades, but leave it to Henry to add a life-saving component to his. Henry sent along this news clipping written by Nancy Smith of the Plano Star Quarterly: "Henry Gentry of Henry's Homemade Ice Cream reports that his annual pajama party last Saturday was not only a smashing success because he had 250 of Plano's PJ'd elite, but he had a bloodmobile drive for the first time. Enough blood was donated to save seventy-two lives.

Congratulation, Henry! You are the winner of August's Duel of the Titans PR award! (Joe Greubel won it in July.)

In July/August, Joe pilfered a page from Henry's own playbook. He teamed up with Johnstown's number-one daily, The Tribune Democrat. The occasion? To celebrate "Ice Cream Day" and promote "NIE Day" (Newspapers in Education). The event was a fundraiser to help cover the costs of providing free newspapers to local area schools. Kids also received free balloons.

The Tribune Democrat provided the tent, tables, ice cream cabinets, and lined up volunteer scoopers. Valley Dairy furnished the ice cream and cones. Plant manager Ray Sheets helped teach the volunteers how to dip. Joe was there in his trade mark Ice Cream Joe get-up to entertain the kids.

Valley Dairy received an incredible amount of publicity. Several quarter-page, multi-colored ads appeared in the daily paper and the Sunday issue. They showed Joe's dad, the late Joe Greubel, Sr.,

Stained Glass cone light fixture in Henry Gentry's Texas home.

along with daughter Melissa and granddaughter Lindsay. The magazine reported on "A Taste of Westmoreland," a benefit for Congregation Emanu-El Israel held on the University of Pittsburgh Greensburg, PA, campus.

Of course, Henry was at it, too! He had his popular "Pajama Party/Celebrity Scoop" on June 15, a big hit with the locals. He is organizing Plano's "Annual Fourth of July Parade" this year (sponsored by the Plano Star Courier and presented by Henry's Homemade Ice Cream"). Henry's "Third Annual Pool Party" is scheduled for August 24 at his palatial residence (no thongs, please!).

Ice Cream Joe: THE VALLEY DAIRY STORY

standing next to the familiar ice cream cart wearing his red-striped vest and skimmer hat. There were also pictures of Joe E. as Ice Cream Joe II, posed with a guy in an Uncle Same costume, interacting with the children. A number of dignitaries showed up, and the Tour d' Toon Bicycle Race held the same day (August 21) helped draw a big crowd. Says Joe: "This was a fun day with lots of good PR, and a big day for Ice Cream Joe meeting the kids and adults."

It pays to be friendly with the people at your local newspaper!

NOVEMBER 2002:
JOE AND HENRY STILL AT IT

I had hoped to get through the month without having to use a lot of ink on either Joe Greubel or Henry Gentry. No such luck. Now Henry has thrown down the gauntlet and challenged Joe to an arm wrestle at the upcoming San Diego meeting. Disgusting! What's next? Nude mud wrestling?

Joe sent a quarter-page spread from the Connellsville, PA, Tribune Review. The September 15 headline read: "Local Restaurant Patrons Adjust to New Location." Apparently, this is major news in this town of 10,000 or so.

I finally figured out why newspaper people like to hang out in Valley Dairy's 12 locations scattered around southwestern PA: 1) They like good food and ice cream. 2) They can always find a story angle while relaxing in pleasant surroundings and writing impressive copy without doing a lot of research. For this piece, reporter Carolyn Holland used this story angle: The old Valley Dairy in the Connellsville Shopping Plaza (there since 1971) recently moved to new, larger, upscale digs in a new building. Some of the older patrons were having trouble adjusting because of a "strong emotional attachment to the old location." Donald Small, Harry "Tuffy" Livengood, Adam Benya and George Bordas, have been eating at the original restaurant since it opened. But, they're adjusting to the new place—slowly.

But, wait! Here's another story angle. It seems that store manager Joseph Stacy inscribed Arlene Honeycutt's name on a seat before it was sent out for reupholstering and placement in the new place. Arlene is adjusting to the new building and meeting her morning-break friends, but it's taking time. "I walked past the old Valley Dairy and looked in the window. Tears filled my eyes." So, if you should ever be driving on Route 119 and see a gray-haired senior upending seats, it'll likely be Arlene looking for the one with her name on the bottom.

Oh, yeah! I forgot about Henry! Here is his latest, unsolicited "Brag of the Month." On the front page of the Sunday Food section of the Dallas Morning Star, September 15, the same day as Joe's spread, the headline reads: "Plano Creamery's Confections A Hit With Local Restauranteurs" Then Susan Taylor writes: "Plano residents know that when they have a hankering for rich ice cream, Henry's Homemade Ice Cream is the place to get a cone or other concoctions. The quintessential neighborhood ice cream shop always has at least forty flavors, all made on the premises." Susan goes on the say that 200 local restaurants use Henry's ice cream, and that Henry's is in the class of "luxuriously decadent." (Henry has got this girl snowed!).

DECEMBER 2002:
JOE MISSES A CONVENTION

I gave Joe Greubel a buzz at his corporate headquarters in Latrobe, PA. "I stayed home," he said. So, wife, Virginia, and daughters, Melissa and Mary Jo, represented Valley Dairy. Joe had Virginia call me back, which was OK by me because she's prettier than Joe. (Looks like the family is trying to phase out the old fella).

DECEMBER 2003:
VALLEY DAIRY DOMINATES THE NEWS

The Kittanning Valley Dairy Restaurant was the recent recipient of one of the Outstanding Employer Awards presented by the Indiana County Supported Employment Advisor Council; Joe and Kittanning assistant manager Mark Evans attended. Manager Tammy Stephens, Debby Anderson and the Valley Dairy staff were lauded for accommodating the needs of co-worker Rebecca, an employee with a disability.

The new Valley Dairy Eatery/Ice Creamery in Blairsville, PA, is now open. Naturally, the press was there for a photo shoot. Big picture of Joe and manager Eric Boggs in the local paper. The Tribune Democrat of Johnstown ran a page of pictures of the Valley Dairy Ebensburg Restaurant for no special reason. On slow news days, photographers simply follow Joe around as he checks his various locations.

Also, Joe wrote and told us that May 2004 will be the key month for 100th anniversary of the banana split, invented in 1904 by Dr. David Strickler, a Latrobe pharmacist. Joe is working with a blue-ribbon committee that includes members of the Latrobe Chamber of Commerce, Saint Vincent College and, of course, Valley Dairy. "We have numerous banana split events and promotions planned for 2004, starting with January," Joe says. The Latrobe Historical Society has commissioned the 9th grade, junior high students to design a banana split cancellation stamp for the Latrobe Post Office. Savings bonds will be awarded for the first three winners. The Post Office will use the 1st place design to cancel mail during the month of May. Banana split pins have been designed, one for Latrobe and one for Valley Dairy, and will be sold by the chamber, Valley Dairy Stores, and other businesses.

Bryce Thomson with Melissa Greubel Blystone. Bryce Thomson, a long-time member and past president of the National Ice Cream Retailers Association, worked for Miller Dairy in Eaton Rapids, Michigan for forty years and eventually became president of the company. His Sundae School Newsletter is now included as an insert in NICRA's monthly bulletin. Photo was taken at the Promised Land Dairy Ranch in Texas.

TOPPINGS
SODA JERK JARGON – MOSTLY OBSOLETE

Black and White — Chocolate soda with vanilla ice cream or chocolate malted milk.

Black Bottom — Chocolate ice cream with chocolate topping.

Black Stick — Chocolate ice cream cone.

Bucket — Large scoop.

Burn It and Let It Swim — Ice cream float.

Burn It All the Way — Chocolate malted with chocolate ice cream.

Canary Island Special — Vanilla soda with chocolate ice cream.

Chicago — Pineapple soda.

Drop — A sundae.

Filet — Pie a la mode.

Glob — Just a plain sundae.

Go for A Walk — Take out order.

Hoboken Special — Pineapple soda with chocolate ice cream.

House Boat — Banana split.

In the Hay — Strawberry milkshake.

Patch — Strawberry ice cream.

Through Georgia — Add chocolate syrup.

Van — Vanilla ice cream.

Vanilla — There's a pretty girl out front.

Soda jerks would combine terms. Through the 1940s, customers marveled at their highly entertaining chants: "Shake a crow of patch," (three strawberry milkshakes); "Canary Island Special to Go For a Walk," (Vanilla soda to take out).

From John Lancaster Riordan's "Soda Fountain Lingo,"
California Folklore Quarterly, Volume 4, 1945.

THE GREAT AMERICAN BANANA SPLIT CONTROVERSY

JANUARY 1984 *The Sundae School Newsletter*
BRYCE THOMSON SORTS OUT THE FACTS

Who was the first fountaineer to cut a banana from stem to stern, plop some ice cream on it and call it a "banana split?"

I had been searching for the answer for years; until recently, that is, when three of my most brilliant researchers, Paul Dickson (*The Great American Ice Cream Book*), Ed Marks (*Ice Screamer*), and Joe Greubel, past president of the National Ice Cream Retailers Association, started to unravel the mystery.

Early last year, Paul Dickson sent me a copy of an article on the banana split which appeared in the October, 1906 edition of Soda Fountain Magazine, which had been sent to him by a researcher at the Smithsonian Institute. Last summer, Ed Marks sent along information from the same magazine. A few weeks ago, Joe Greubel sent news clippings relating to the soda jerk who very possibly created the first banana split.

Let's see if I can sort out the facts.

According to the Soda Fountain Magazine piece, "…the banana split first came into public notice at the Boston convention of the N.A.R.D., which I think means National Association of Retail Druggists.

The article continues. "One of the features of the Boston convention was the hospitality which was offered by the manufacturers and supply houses, yet among all the beverages dispensed here, none was more novel with the ladies than the banana split."

A young man named Stinson Thomas, a "chief dispenser at Butler's Department Store" of Boston, seems to have promoted the banana split in a big way, as we may gather from the following passage:

My trade here is always looking for something new,' said Mr. Thomas the other day to a representative of The Soda Fountain, and the thought occurred to me that I might prepare a popular fountain beverage with the banana. I sent my boy out to buy a half dozen of bananas, and when he returned I cut off the ends of a banana, split it open, put a portion of ice cream on top and a spoonful of crushed strawberries. It certainly looked swell, and I believed the public would like it. I began with a dozen bananas a day, and when a customer appeared to be in doubt as to what to order, I suggested a banana split. If the dozen bananas were not used up in a day, I instructed my dispensers to prepare banana splits and give them away. It is a little more than a year now since the banana split was introduced here, and it is easily our fountain leader. We use four or five bunches of bananas a day, and people come for miles to get it. At first we left the peel on the banana in the plate, but some time ago we began removing it altogether. We found the ladies preferred to have the peel removed. As we serve the banana split today, we take a whole banana, remove the peel, and then split the banana lengthwise, and lay it on a plate. On top of it we put two small scoops of ice cream, generally vanilla. The on top of each portion of ice cream we put a red cherry, with a few slices of peach between them. Half a teaspoon of pistachio and half a teaspoon of crushed walnuts sprinkled over the top completes the dish. As I said before, that is our great leader. In the busy hours of the day I am able to do little else beside splitting bananas for the dispensers.

Just when I was about to establish the 1905 N.A.R.D. Boston convention as the birthplace of the banana split, Joe Greubel gets into act by sending along local news clippings which claim that a soda jerk working in a Latrobe, PA, drugstore by the name of David Strickler, concocted the first banana split in 1904.

According to a Greensburg (PA) *Tribune-Review* article (May 5, 1980), "It happened in 1904 when a young David Strickler was learning the drug business in the Tassell Pharmacy which later became Strickler's."

His daughter told the *Tribune-Review* that her dad was "always a great experimenter." She added, "There were no dishes for the concoction, so he drew up his own and had the people in Grapeville [a glass factory in Jeannette, PA] design it."

The original Strickler banana split as reported by the *Tribune-Review* consisted of three scoops of hand-dipped ice cream, a whole banana cut lengthwise, chocolate syrup, marshmallow, whipped cream, nuts, and a plump cherry, all for ten cents.

Another of Joe Greubel's clippings—one by Jack George in his "Sidewalk Soundings" from the Latrobe Community Edition of the *Tribune-Review* (November 10, 1983)—states:

> Many years ago [George was well into his eighties at the time he wrote the column] the late Charlie Poorman, who bought Strickler's Drug Store, invited me up to a camp in Cameron County for the weekend, and among those present was Doctor Dave Strickler. We

Patrons enjoy ice cream delights at the Philadelphia Exposition, 1876, the year that the banana was introduced to American consumers. (Courtesy: National Archives)

all gathered around a wood fire in the evening and were engaged in some small talk when Doctor Strickler told how he came about the idea of a banana split. It was an interesting story, and when we returned home we wrote about the trip in my column, and we've written about it several times since.

A formula for the banana split is also listed in some copies of *The American Soda Book*, which was first published by James W. Tufts in 1863, and was the soda dispenser's bible for about fifty years. Since the book went through many editions (and we must assume revisions) during the decades that followed, we have no way of knowing when the banana-split formula was added. It certainly did not appear in any editions before 1876, since the United Fruit Company did not introduce the banana to American consumers until that year at the Philadelphia Exposition. A Cleveland Fruit Juice Company "Prices to the Trade for 1910" is stapled to my copy, which indicates that the formula was added at least by that year.

Here is the formula:

> Peel and split a banana, lay both halves on the bottom of a large saucer, on the top of the banana put a once-shaped measure of ice cream, over this pour a little crushed pineapple, a little whole strawberry, and a spoonful of whipped cream, and top with a cherry.

Following this formula, the book lists another interesting sundae called, "Banana Sundae a la Delmonico" and the formula for its making:

> Spread a small, fresh fern leaf on a saucer, then take a banana, lay it on, cut open at the top so it works as a hinge; spread it out, put on a ladle of vanilla ice cream, a ladle of whipped cream, and lastly pour over it an ounce of prunelle brandy. This is new brandy cordial. If it is not obtainable, use crème de coco."

And so, fellow Banana Splitters, we hope we have cleared up some of the mystery for you about the birth of the banana split.

Until someone comes up with new evidence, we give Doc Strickler credit for concocting the first one in 1904. Though other cities might claim credit for the first banana split, Doc Strickler certainly leads the field as the inventor, as a simple Internet search will show, and his drugstore in Latrobe, PA as the place where he first served it.

Aside from anything else, Oneida credits him with the invention and with designing the first banana-split dish. I also seems that he was the first to include three flavors of ice cream, rather than plain vanilla. No matter that several banana-type ice cream concoctions might have been invented in various places, it seems clear that Dr. Strickler gave us our classic banana split, today an American institution.

JANUARY 24, 2002
Clinton County, Ohio News Release

IT'S WILMINGTON, OHIO VS. LATROBE, PENNSYLVANIA & IT'S ALL OVER FOOD!

It's become a major topic of debate in two neighboring states - Ohio and Pennsylvania - and it's all over food. It may sound silly, but to Wilmington, Ohio it's an issue worth fighting for, if only figuratively. The food in question is the all-American banana split, and the debate itself is over who first "invented" this well-know ice cream dessert.

After nearly a century of hearing how the banana split received its birth, the people of Wilmington went so far as to preserve the claim, that they created a festival in its name. The Banana Split Festival is now in its eighth year. Ever increasing exposure for the festival brought Latrobe, Pennsylvania's claim to surface last year. Their claim boasts of its creation two years prior to Wilmington's, but it's a claim Wilmington refuses to accept.

The people of Wilmington stand by their claim and even brought the family of the dessert's creator, Ernest Hazard, to the Banana Split Festival two years ago to recognize his role in influencing Americana. Hazard's grandson and daughter recall the story exactly as it's been told for decades. Here's the story.

In downtown Wilmington, there used to be a restaurant called Hazard's. The proprietor of the restaurant was Ernest Hazard. Like most merchants in Wilmington today he wanted to find a way to

Hazard's Restaurant in Wilmington, Ohio, 1905. Sadly, Hazard's discovered the banana split one year after Dr. David Strickler served the first one in Latrobe, Pennsylvania.

attract the students of Wilmington College to come to his restaurant.

It was a very blustery winter in 1907, so business was slow and the employees didn't have a whole lot of work to do. So Hazard decided that a good way to get some business was to create a new dish that was so unique everyone would want to try it. So he offered to furnish unlimited ingredients to the employees and have a contest to see who could come up with the most unusual dish.

Surprisingly enough, the winner of the contest was Ernest Hazard. He took a long dessert dish, arranged a peeled banana and three scoops of ice cream in it, and added a shot of chocolate syrup, a little strawberry jam, and a few bits of pineapple. On top of this, he sprinkled some ground nuts, and garnished his invention with a mountain of whipped cream and two red cherries on its peak.

After winning the contest Hazard faced another dilemma. What would he name the dish? Some help was needed with this aspect of public relations, so Hazard enlisted the opinion of his cousin, Clifton Hazard, for the job.

Hazard made the concoction for Clifton and asked him to take a taste test. He then told him that he had an idea in mind for the name, a banana split. Upon hearing that, Clifton told him that he didn't think that the name was one that would help him get any extra publicity. He didn't think that anyone would ever walk in and ask for something called a banana split.

There are those who might dispute Wilmington's claim, but nevertheless, thousands of people will flock to Wilmington to sample an old-fashioned banana split during the second weekend in June. They'll also hear the story that has endured the years of how Hazard created the first banana split.

JUNE 03, 2001
Chuck Martin, *The Cincinnati Enquirer*

LATROBE, PA., AND WILMINGTON BOTH CLAIM THIS SUNDAE STARTED IN THEIR TOWN

Maybe we should let this one alone.

It's the case of two small towns — Wilmington, Ohio, and Latrobe, Pa. — that claim to be the birthplace of one of the oldest ice cream sundaes — the banana split.

The town's split on who created the decadent dessert first. And to make it more sticky — even though residents of Wilmington and Latrobe have bragged about their homegrown treat for years — they say they've never heard of their rival's claim.

Folks in Wilmington, about fifty miles northeast of Cincinnati in Clinton County, say restaurant owner Ernest Hazard created the banana split in the blustery winter of 1907. Business was slow, the story goes, so Mr. Hazard devised the sundae — made with a split banana, ice cream, fruit, chocolate toppings, whipped cream, crushed nuts and maraschino

Popular magazines frequently featured banana splits, as they do today. *Courtesy Ed Marks.*

Inserts: Commemorative banana split pins created in Latrobe to celebrate the 100th anniversary of the invention of the banana split. A lady's fan of the 1920s and 1930s. The traditional three-scoop banana split has been suggestively altered.

1947 Soda Jerk's Guide to Banana Splits.
Courtesy: Ice Cream Merchandising Institute

Ice Cream Joe: THE VALLEY DAIRY STORY

cherry — as a way to attract students from nearby Wilmington College.

Many in Wilmington grew up hearing the story, and naturally assumed the banana split's home was their birthright. Dan Rodenfels always believed it, even though his grandfather — Mr. Hazard — died when he was young.

"It was what my mother (Roberta Hazard Rodenfels) told me," says Mr. Rodenfels, publisher of the Logan Daily News, near Athens. "And she made me plenty of banana splits when I was a kid."

Proud of its banana split heritage, Wilmington began celebrating the birth of the sundae seven years ago with an annual festival in June. This year, Wilmington's Banana Split Festival will be Friday and Saturday in J.W. Denver Williams Memorial Park.

"I do believe there is a bigger awareness of banana splits here," says Mary Gibson, who owns Gibson's Goodies ice cream shop in Wilmington and provides ice cream for the festival. Last year, Ms. Gibson sold more than 2,000 banana splits during the two-day event.

But the Latrobe story predates Ohio's.

About 275 miles away in western Pennsylvania, the residents of Latrobe always have heard the story of how optometrist Dr. David Strickler invented the banana split at his downtown pharmacy. According to legend, Dr. Strickler was inspired while watching soda jerks work during a visit to Atlantic City, N.J. He came home to create the banana split in 1904 — three years before Mr. Hazard supposedly unveiled his sundae in Wilmington.

Like Mr. Hazard, Dr. Strickler was motivated in part by marketing. He hoped his banana split would draw students from nearby St. Vincent College. It worked: The college students loved the sundae and spread word about it when they returned home, mostly on the East Coast. The banana split became so popular, Dr. Strickler asked a local glass company to custom-make a long, narrow dish to hold his ice cream creation.

"We were the originators of the banana split," declares Carl Mattioli, president of the Latrobe Historical Society.

Mr. Mattioli also points out that the town of about 9,000 is the home of Rolling Rock Beer, Fred "Mr." Rogers, and the first professional football game.

"We should have the (Pro) Football Hall of Fame here, but people here sat on their haunches too long and Canton (Ohio) got it," Mr. Mattioli says.

So you can bet the people of Latrobe don't want to give up their claims on the banana split, especially to an Ohio town.

Latrobe takes its sundae history seriously — the town's Elks Club has a banana split on its official pin, and St. Vincent College uses the banana split story in its recruiting material. Latrobe doesn't hold a banana split festival like Wilmington does, but the town is planning an event for 2004, celebrating the split's 100th anniversary. Of course, Wilmington will mark the anniversary three years later.

"I do believe we were first," says Joe Greubel, owner of the Valley Dairy ice cream chain in Latrobe. "I knew Dr. Strickler. And I still regret not having my picture taken with him."

A more objective expert, Bryce Thomson, who lives in Eaton Rapids, Mich., and claims to be the "world's oldest soda jerk" at age 84 (now 87), sides with Latrobe in the banana split dispute.

"I have never heard about Wilmington's claim," says Mr. Thomson, who has written the Sundae School Newsletter for the Ice Cream Retailers Association for 20 years. "Most historians agree Latrobe is the home of the banana split."

But Wilmington isn't backing down.

"Our research indicates that Wilmington remains the birthplace of the banana split as we know it today," says Debbie Stamper of the Clinton County Convention & Visitors Bureau.

Since both alleged creators have long since died, their respective businesses have closed and no living relatives can make undisputed claims, mysteries surrounding the birth of the banana split will continue. Bananas became popular in the United States around the turn of the 20th century, but how could two men create two such unusual sundaes that looked so much alike?

Ice Cream Joe: THE VALLEY DAIRY STORY

To make things more intriguing, a published report documents the introduction of something called the "banana split" in 1905 by a department store soda jerk at a convention of the National Association of Retail Druggists in Boston. Did the soda jerk learn to concoct the banana split from Dr. Strickler, or did Dr. Strickler learn from him and then fudge the date of his creation? Did Mr. Hazard attend the same convention and return home to Wilmington to "invent" the banana split two years later?

"Who knows?" says his grandson, Mr. Rodenfels. "And who cares?"

The Oneida Company
BANANA SPLIT PERFECTION

They called themselves "Perfectionists." As a group of rebellious Calvinists, they settled in 1848 near Oneida Creek in Central New York.

Their religious and social experiment substituted the small home and family unit for a group family, where the interest of one member became the interest of all. And so, as the Community went about the business of earning a living, it was very properly a group effort.

At first, silver knives, forks and spoons were made in accordance with their strict standards of perfection. And, as the business grew and prospered, the Oneida Community earned a reputation for elegant but also very practical table pieces. Although the Community officially dissolved in 1880, the business born of that noble experiment was carried on under the name of Oneida.

It was in the summer of 1904 that David "Doc" Strickler first sliced a banana down the middle, added scoops of differently-flavored ice creams, and embellished the top with an interplay of fruit toppings. In the prosperity of post-World War II America, indulgent Banana Splits enjoyed renewed popularity, and Oneida honored the dessert with a Footed, Stainless-Steel Banana Boat that has been the standard for Banana Split service for nearly half a century.

Although these classic Banana Boats are no longer in production, The NEW YORK FIRST Company has been invited to offer the remaining pieces of this quintessential soda fountain masterpiece.

JULY 4, 1999
Joe Blundo, *Columbus Ohio Dispatch*
FIRST BANANA SPLIT?

In 1904, the story goes, a customer entered the soda fountain at Foeller's Drug Store, 567 N. Nigh St., and asked Letty Lally for "something different."

Lally responded with a banana-and-ice-cream concoction that quickly caught on. Thus did Columbus give the world the banana split.

[**Editor's note**: Bryce Thomson's remarks concerning Letty Lally (*Sundae School Newsletter*, October 2002) – "Who whipped up the first Banana Royal (any sundae with banana slices)?" I'm giving that credit to Columbus soda jerk Letty Lally, who made a sundae with banana slices in 1904. Later, Columbus, Ohio, promoters got the bright idea of touting it as the first banana split. Because of Letty's catchy name, she belongs in the history books, so I'm saying she invented the first Banana Royal. I'd sure like to meet that gal . . . Ooops! . . . on second thought, she'd be about 120 years old by now"].

Maybe. The story is a nice one, said Betty Davis, founder and president of the National Association of Soda Jerks. The problem: Lots of other towns have similar stories. "I've heard every community across the nation say they founded the banana split," she said. One constant in all the stories: They originate around the turn of the century, according to Davis. An Iowa town claims an enterprising merchant invented the split there when he tried to figure out what to do with ripe bananas. The Chicago Tribune, in a 1994 story on the 90th birthday of the banana split, said its invention usually is credited to David Strickler of Strickler's Pharmacy in Latrobe, Pa., in 1904.

Other accounts say a man named Stinson Thomas made the split in Boston in 1905. Proving who really invented the banana split is impossible, Davis said. "If you want to claim it in Columbus, it's fine with me."

"1ST" BANANA SPLIT
DR. DAVID STRICKLER
"1904"

Saint Vincent College students line up to make their own banana splits. Banana splits are the usual fare at student gatherings, parents' days, and on any other justifiable occasion. It is generally believed that students from the college were responsible for introducing the banana split to their hometowns in 1904 when they returned to them during semester breaks.

Ice Cream Joe: THE VALLEY DAIRY STORY

A Valley Dairy waitress serves up three Valley Dairy banana splits.

Joe E. Greubel with Dr. David Strickler's grandson.

Left: Joe E. Greubel with Tom Lazarchik, last owner/operator of Strickler's Drug Store on Ligonier Street, Latrobe, Pennsylvania. Dr. Strickler was a clerk there in 1904, when he invented the banana split, as we know it today. Strickler also contracted with a Jeannette, Pennsylvania, glass manufacturer make a specially shaped dish, one of the hallmarks of the way today's banana splits are served.

Jack Michaels of Johnstown PA Morning DJ for WKYE with Jim McTavish.

Ice Cream Joe: THE VALLEY DAIRY STORY

BANANA SPLIT BASH IN LATROBE

Melissa Greubel Blystone serves banana splits at Legion Keener Park in Latrobe, Pennsylvania, for a Concert in the Park and Banana Split Bash.

Key:
1 — Banana Halves
2 — Assorted Ice Creams
3 — Assorted Toppings
4 — Whipped Cream
5 — Chopped Nuts
6 — Maraschino Cherries

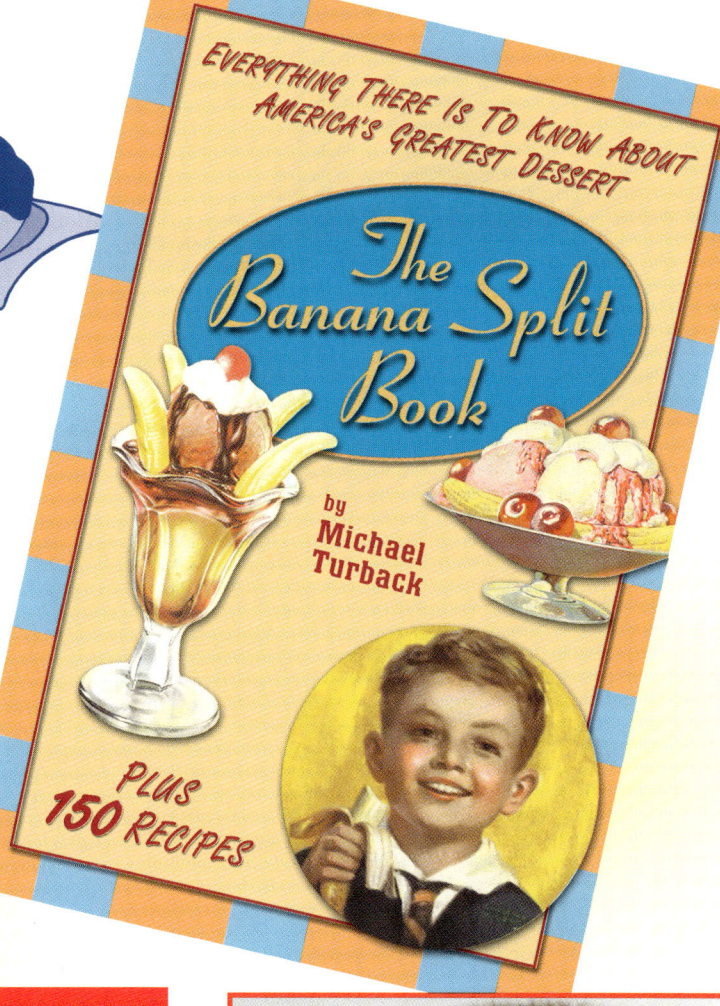

Mike Turback wrote his definitive The Banana Split Book: Everything There Is to Know About America's Greatest Dessert in time for what he calls "The Year of the Split," the 100th anniversary of the invention of the banana split in Latrobe, Pennsylvania, in 1904.

As he says: "In 1904, a soda fountain apprentice in Latrobe, Pennsylvania, took a ripe banana, cut it lengthwise, laid it out on an elliptical dish, smothered it with ice cream, marshmallow, maraschino cherries, pineapple slices and crushed nuts, then topped the whole shebang with sweet syrups that oozed down the sides to envelop the banana protruding at the base. It was a preposterous concoction, and one that vaulted him into immortality."

Turback goes on to say: "The banana split is not only American by birth, it reflects our genius for invention, passion for indulgence, and reputation for wackiness. It's like no other dessert in the world -- a grand idea that could only be conceived in a place as grand as America."

Mike Turback operated an award-winning restaurant, Turback's of Ithaca, New York, for nearly three decades. His first book A Month of Sundaes, brought him instant recognition as one of the country's leading authorities on ice cream history.

Ice Cream Joe: THE VALLEY DAIRY STORY

BANANA SPLIT CENTENNIAL STATION
JULY 2, 2004
LATROBE, PA 15650

The Latrobe Post Office's commemoration cancellation stamp for the month of July 2004, celebrating the 100th Anniversary of the invention of the banana split.

The "Centennial Split," a watercolor by Peg Panasiti commissioned by the Greubel family and Valley Dairy for the banana split's 100th anniversary.

A Letter to I've Got a Secret
From Dr. David E. Strickler, September 10, 1959

Gentlemen:

My secret is that "I Made the First Banana Split."

In the year 1904, as a young boy learning the drug business in the Tassell Pharmacy, Latrobe, PA (later Strickler's Drug Store), I made the first banana split.

A price of 10¢ was set for the item at that time. Now it can be bought nearly all over the world and sells for as high as $1.00.

The promotion of banana splits over the country was made through a clerk in the Tassell Pharmacy, the late Dr. Howard Dovey. Dr. Dovey practiced medicine in Everett and Mercersburg, PA, for many years. It was when Mr. Dovey was in medical school in Philadelphia that he told other students about the big hit this delicious concoction was making in Latrobe. He showed them how it was made in the long, narrow dish especially made for this purpose. These students in turn taught soda fountain clerks, on their vacation trips, in that great resort city, Atlantic City, New Jersey. Soon it was a popular item on the menu of most soda fountains in the U.S.A. and spread to countries outside the country.

It warms my heart to look back and remember that "I made the very first banana split" in a little drug store in a little town.

For verification, may I refer you to our Burgess, Mr. Victor B. Stader.

I hope you will enjoy, and maybe use, my big secret to entertain the TV audience of your interesting program.

Sincerely,

Dr. David E. Strickler

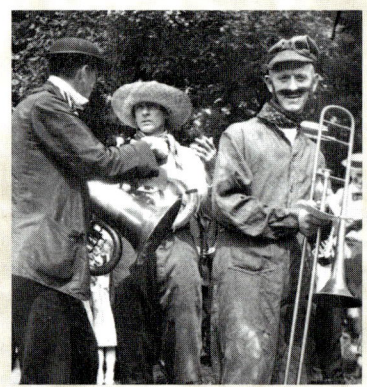

Pictured left to right: Susan Skoloda (Commercial Bank), Katie Knupp, Stacie Venzin, Joe E. Greubel, T.J. Valore. In the foreground is Cassie Trumbetta.

BANANA SPLIT POSTER CONTEST 2004

Cassie Trumbetta

Kati Knupp

Stacie Venzin

T.J. Valore

In honor of the 100th Anniversary of the Banana Split and the 70th Anniversary of Commercial Bank of Pennsylvania, Valley Dairy and Commercial Bank sponsored a poster-drawing contest.

The contest was open to any student in the Latrobe area and the drawing was to represent the anniversaries of the Banana Split and Commercial Bank of Pennsylvania. 302 entries were received.

Commercial Bank awarded the winners with a $500 Savings Bond while Valley Dairy issued a certificate for a free Banana Split. The Latrobe Chamber of Commerce provided banana split pins.

Winners were: Katie Knupp, Latrobe Elementary School; Cassie Trumbetta, Christ The Divine; T.J. Valore, Christ The Divine and Stacie Venzin, Latrobe Senior High.

Ice Cream Joe: THE VALLEY DAIRY STORY

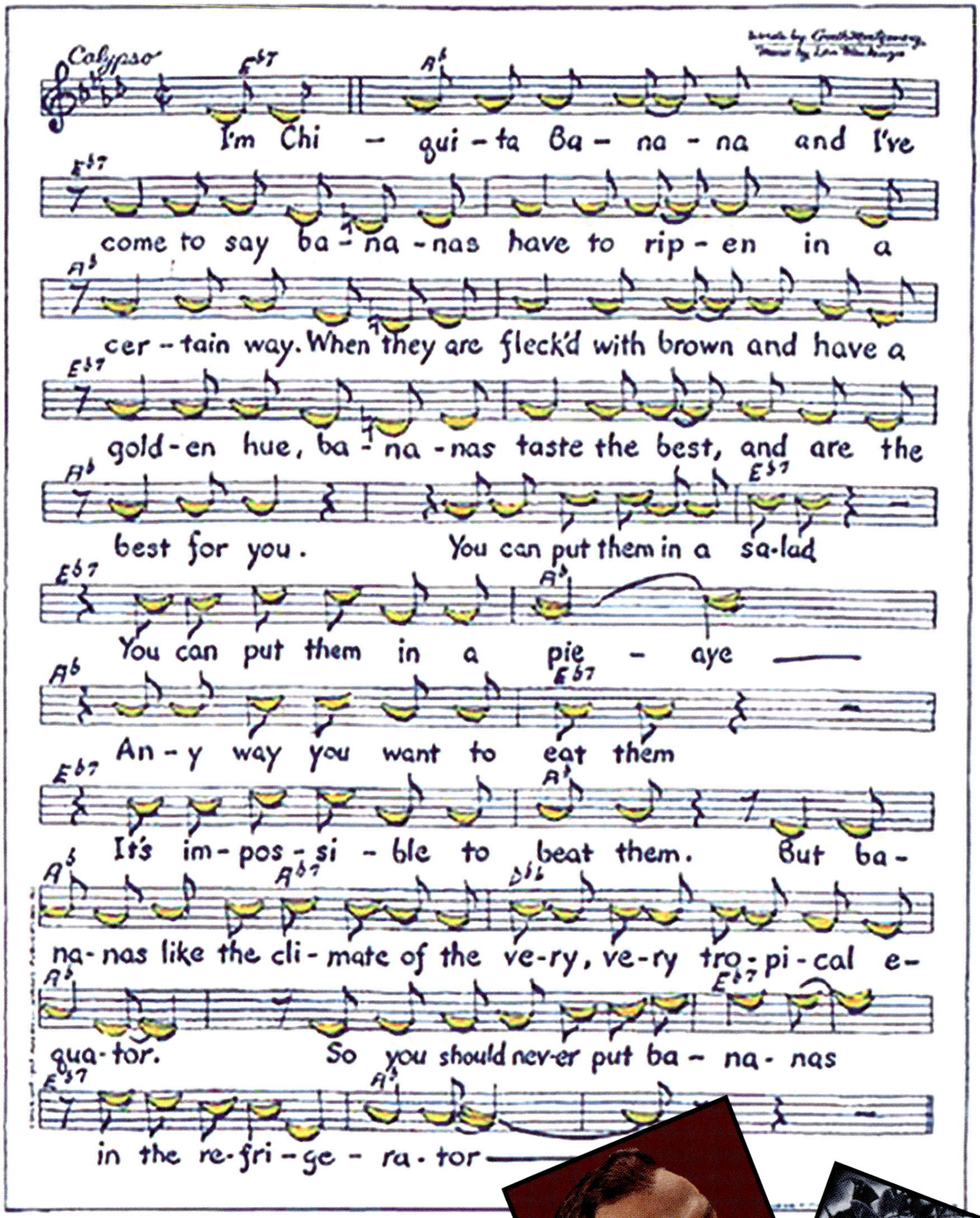

The Chiquita Banana Song was immortalized by Latin American entertainers Carmen Miranda and Xavier Cugat, and was as popular in the 1940s as any song that made the Hit Parade. Garth Montgomery wrote and words, and Len MacKenzi wrote the music.

"I would rather play "Chiquita Banana" and have my swimming pool, than play Bach and starve." – Xavier Cugat

Ice Cream Joe: THE VALLEY DAIRY STORY

WHO IS THE LITTLE GIRL IN THE PICTURE?

"Back in 1984, an adorable little four-year-old girl with golden blond ringlets was being bribed wih ice cream sodas to pose for the now widely recognized photos that appear in the Valley Dairy stores. Aside from every child's dream of having all the ice cream she could want, she could also brag to her friends that 'I was in advertising with Ice Cream Joe!' Today, that little girl, Shannon Welling of McCandless Township, is a senior at Indiana University of Pennsylvania. She still enjoys ice cream at Valley Dairy and proudly tells her friends, " I'm the girl in the pictures!'"

—A note from Phil Welling, 2004

Shannon Welling

Ice Cream Joe: THE VALLEY DAIRY STORY

YOU CAN'T MISS WITH KIDS

Left: 1969. Andy Stuchal, Margaret Greubel sit opposite Dave and Lori Campbell, enjoying burgers and sundaes at the Indiana, Pennsylvania, Valley Dairy.

DEAR JOE,

"Enclos'd is a photo of our grandson, Aiden Miller. Whenever we finish our Valley Dairy ice cream, we can't throw the carton away! Aiden runs for it and plays so hard with it on his head. Thought you might get a kick out of this!"

- Bill and Ethel Gasper

Ice Cream Joe: THE VALLEY DAIRY STORY

"Ah, but you haven't seen the ice pudding," said Cook. "Come along." Why was she being so nice, though Sun as she gave them each a hand. And they looked into the refrigerator.

Oh! Oh! Oh! It was a little house. It was a little pink house with white snow on the roof and green windows and a brown door and stuck in the door there was a nut for a handle.

"Let me touch it. Just let me put my finger on the roof," said Moon, dancing. She always wanted to touch all the food. Sun didn't...

... And the little pink house with the snow roof and the green windows was broken — broken — half melted away in the center of the table.

"Come on, Sun," said Father, pretending not to notice . . .

"Daddy, Daddy," shrieked Moon. "The little handle is left. The little nut. Can I eat it?"

And she ran across and picked it out of the door and scrunched it up, biting hard and blinking...

Sun and Moon, Katherine Mansfield.

107

SERVICE WITH A SMILE!

Ice Cream Joe: THE VALLEY DAIRY STORY

ICE CREAM JOE –
WAS ALWAYS READY WITH A HUG, LIVELY CONVERSATION...

Ice Cream Joe: THE VALLEY DAIRY STORY

...AND SOME DELICIOUS SAMPLES

Ice Cream Joe: THE VALLEY DAIRY STORY

Happy 100th Birthday!

Margaret Steele's 100th birthday. Ice Cream Joe presented her with a surprise banana split. She dug in, but spit out the nuts. Left to right: Margaret's nieces Dorothy Randolph, Lillian Sloan, Phyllis Smith.

YOU'LL NEVER SEE YOUR SQUIRREL AGAIN

D. Black (left), Director of the Humane Society of Cambria County, and Andrea Hess of the Valley Dairy Richland store, read a note from "Bucky."

Workers at Valley Dairy in Richland Township were going nuts with worry after discovering a beloved stuffed squirrel had been kidnapped and was being held for ransom.

Just after Christmas (2003), Andrea Hess, who manages the store at 1224 Scalp Avenue, received the first ransom letter regarding the five-inch animal's disappearance.

"The perpetrator sent a note demanding free coffee for life," Hess said in a telephone interview as she told of the squirrel's saga.

The "kidnapper" referred to the stuffed animal as "Bucky," and enclosed a photograph of the rodent - blindfolded.

"Free coffee for life or the squirrel gets it," the letter stated. So Hess and her staff decided to offer a small reward for anyone who would supply a lead for Bucky's safe return.

As donations and leads began pouring in, a second letter was received, this time postmarked from Steubenville, Ohio.

"The letter said Bucky had a girlfriend and his own apartment, and not to worry about him, because he was doing fine," she said, laughing. The second letter also came with a photo, this time with Bucky with his arm around a little blonde doll.

Meanwhile, leads came trickling in, along with donations that amassed in excess of $200.00.

"When we realized we had collected a lot more money than what we had anticipated, we decided to make a deal," Hess explained. "We decided to donate the reward money to the Humane Society of Cambria County in exchange for Bucky's safe return, no questions asked."

Hess put a sign in front of the collection cup at the restaurant to get he word out about the deal, and, shortly thereafter, she received a telephone call from D. Black, executive director of the humane society.

"The squirrel was delivered in a box addressed to us, and Bucky was inside, complete with his travel bag and a blanket to keep him warm," Black said in a telephone interview.

The box had a Mount Pleasant, Westmoreland County, postmark on it.

Black promptly turned custody over to Hess, who, in turn, presented the Humane Society with a $225.00 check.

Although Hess stressed that no charges would be filed, as part of the agreement for Bucky's safe return, she has narrowed the kidnapper down to a trucker [a Valley Dairy regular patron] known only as "Mike," who drives [for a food service].

"We're not supposed to know it was him," Hess said. "We're just glad he did the right thing and returned Bucky to us."

- Julie Benamati
Johnstown Tribune-Democrat

Ice Cream Joe: THE VALLEY DAIRY STORY

VALLEY DAIRY

Valley Dairy
A Place in Town
A Meeting spot
For All Around.

A cup of coffee
A burger or fries
Good Conversation
With all the guys.

The waitresses are friendly
Your cup is never empty
The atmosphere cozy
It sure is tempty.

So if your're in the vicinity
And want to spend some time
Valley Dairy is the place
No other like its kind.

-Arlene Honeycut. Connellsville, Pennsylvania

LIKE FATHER – LIKE SON

Top: Ice Cream Joe with State Representative Jess Stairs at a Latrobe Fourth of July parade.

Center: Ice Cream Joe with Bob Rose and Dean Rose at the Connellsville, Pennsylvania, Valley Dairy.

Bottom: Ice Cream Joe with Professor and Mrs. Donald Reilly of the University of Pittsburgh at Greensburg's Humanities Department, at the Connellsville Valley Dairy.

Ice Cream Joe: THE VALLEY DAIRY STORY

Top left: Ice Cream Joe with a clown, who said, "Do you know the one thing grizzly bears will not eat? Clowns… because they taste funny."

Ice Cream Joe with Mrs. Pennsylvania in Johnstown, Pennsylvania, for Newspapers in Education Day (on behalf of the Johnstown Tribune-Democrat)

Chick Cicconi of Ligonier, Pennsylvania, with Ice Cream Joe. Cicconi played Uncle Sam in Latrobe's Fourth of July Parades.

Joe E. Greubel in "civilian clothes" with Bill and Nell Strickler at the Latrobe Route 30 Shopping Center Valley Dairy.

Photos below: Ice Cream Joe in "uniform" with an array of customers.

Ice Cream Joe: THE VALLEY DAIRY STORY

TOPPINGS

Back in the mid-1960s, we had small office right off the plant store in Windber. From in there it was easy to see and hear customers out in the store. In the food business the price of the cup of coffee is quite a sensitive item. In the ice cream business it's half gallons. I sat in that office night after night laboring over increased mix cost, packaging cost, and other things. I was trying to do my very best to only make a minimal price raise in the retail price of a half gallon of ice cream. Night after night I labored and sweated on the thing and, finally, I reached a decision. It was a modest price increase. Nevertheless, it was an increase, and I was a little bit concerned that it might affect our sales. The first evening of the increase, I'm sitting in the office when a customer came in, walked over to the counter, and put a half-gallon of ice cream at the register. The clerk said, "You know, the price went up today on those half gallons." I told the clerks to tell customers that, rather than just collecting the money. The fellow looked at her and said, "Hey, it doesn't matter. Valley Dairy is the only kind of ice cream my dog will eat." After that, I quit worrying about price increases.

I inherited from Dad the desire to do whatever necessary to please our customers. Sometimes the pressure made me a little nervous. When I was young and working in one of the stores, I got busy putting together a banana split for one of our regulars. Vanilla, chocolate, strawberry. Whipped cream. Fruit toppings. Cherry. Nuts. I stepped back and admired my work. A perfect job, or so I thought. When the customer had finished, I collected his dish and asked, "How was everything?" He answered, "Great. It would have been an even better banana split, except for one thing." "Oh, and what's that?" "Next time, don't forget to put in the banana!"

- Joe E. Greubel

CREATING, PROMOTING, SELLING
TECHNOLOGY, SUPPLY, DEMAND

An 1884 poster advertising an "Ice Cream Social." The ice cream social was a popular event in the latter part of the nineteenth century and the early decades of the twentieth. Courtesy of Ed Marks.

For most of its mythical and real history, ice cream remained a delicacy of the rich and privileged. All of that would change in 1851 when Jacob Fussell, a Baltimore milkman, realized that he could profit by using his excess cream to make ice cream, then charging twenty-five cents a quart, some forty cents less than the leading ice cream producers of his day. It wasn't long before ice cream was making him more money than his milk sales.

Fussell's business blossomed, and by 1864 he was making ice cream in New York at a price the "common folk" could afford. It wasn't long before he came into conflict with the Associated Confectioners of New York who tried to force him into signing a contract in which he would agree to sell his ice cream at $1.25 or $1.00 if the patrons bought directly at the site and did not require delivery. Fussell, of course, refused. In 1869, Stephen Dunnington, Nathaniel Woodhill and James Horton, who founded the Horton Ice Cream Company in New York in 1864, joined Fussell as partners. Their prices were revolutionary - $1.00 per gallon for hotel restaurants, community and church events. Other entities could purchase ice cream at quantity discounts starting at $1.00 per gallon over five gallons and $1.20 per gallon under five gallons.

For most of the United States in the 1880s, the typical ice cream plant used a large, hand-cranked freezer to make ice cream, an undoubtedly tedious, and time-consuming process. By 1900, the ice cream industry began to grow into the giant we know today. Between 1900 and 1920, sales went from five million gallons to 150 million.

A 10" x 12" Dixie Cup point-of-sale poster. Courtesy of Ed Marks.

Promoters were quick to point out the health benefits of eating ice cream as this poster promo of the late 1930s suggests. Not only the heroic characters of fiction, but also the actors who played them in films, were enlisted to promote ice cream as a health food. In this case, it is Johnny Weissmuller, an Olympic Gold Medallist in swimming, seems to be slaying the leopard. Courtesy of Ed Marks.

National Food." And it was that, if the decision of immigration authorities to serve ice cream to newly arriving immigrants at Ellis Island is any proof.

The public could buy ice cream almost anywhere, but especially at the "Soda Fountain," a new American institution, along with the ice cream soda, the sundae, the banana split, and, above all, that icon of American popular culture, the Soda Jerk, a figure as equally talented as another American icon, the Bartender, a personality blessed with a sympathetic ear, juggling talents, and expertise in psychological counseling.

During the Great Depression ice cream sales dropped by half, despite the optimism of the editors of The Ice Cream Review in an issue dated before the stock market crash of October 1929. When Prohibition was repealed in 1933 with the passage of the Twenty-first Amendment, ice creamers became alarmed the alcoholic beverages, now readily available, would reduce ice cream sales even further. The industry had already suffered because of the advent of more-affordable home refrigerators and efficient portable ice cream freezers. These made making ice cream at home a viable proposi-

New inventions were responsible for the growth - the specialized utilization of steam power, the homogenizer, electric motors, automated packaging machines, new refrigeration and freezing processes, the refrigerated motor-truck. By 1920, most of the modern processes of ice cream making were in place, and the ice cream plant pretty much resembled those of today. The same was true of marketing strategies of the day - advertisements in magazines, newspapers, trade journals, in the movie theatres and on radio, the use of celebrity testimonials, office supplies (ink blotters were a specialty), calendars, trading cards, plates, serving trays, post cards, popular music, collectibles, holiday promotions, and many other extant or created avenues.

Enterprising publishers created The Ice Cream Review and The Ice Cream Trade Journal. Ice cream making became a household possibility with the advent of the home ice cream maker. Advertisers created slogans like "Ice Cream - The

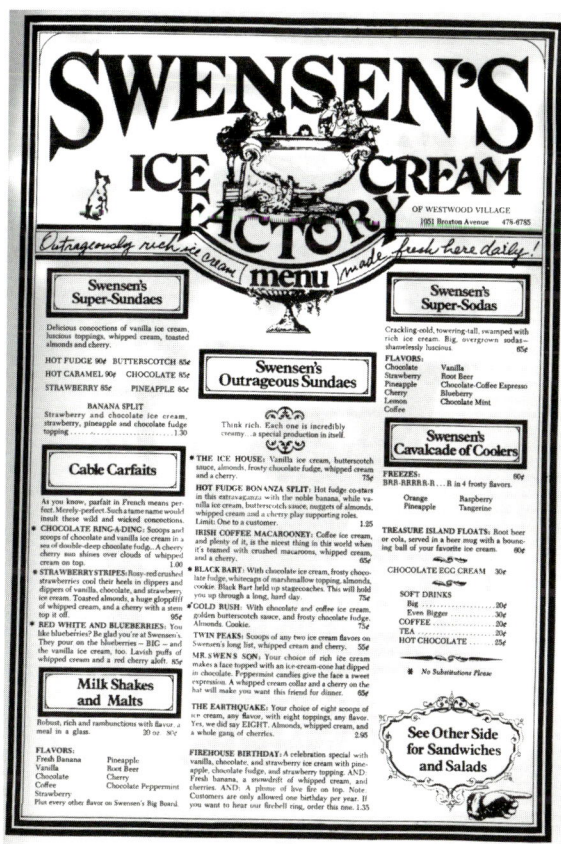

1970s Swenson of San Francisco menu created in an antique mode and advertising the company's varied flavors. As the twentieth century progressed, scores of flavors appeared on the market, including Bryce Thomson's "Dill Pickle." Other flavors, most of them extinct, included: mashed potato and bacon, tuna fish, fried pork rind, chili con carne, garlic, sauerkraut, horseradish and beer, mustard, dill pickle, ketchup.

Ice Cream Joe: THE VALLEY DAIRY STORY

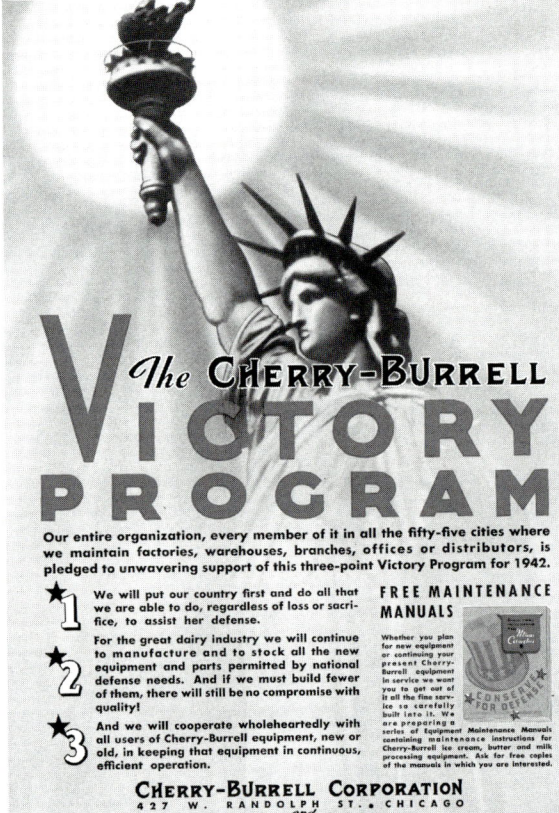

tion, and Mom and Pop retailers could make ice cream virtually at the counter, selling it as "homemade."

By the mid-thirties, the industry was making a comeback with new and creative marketing ideas. The industry, more than ever, use the ethical appeal that celebrated actors and entertainers could provide. Fred Astaire and Ginger Rogers teamed up with Borden's to advertise the "Hollywood Lunch," a milkshake and sandwich. More than 25,000 soda fountains displayed a scene from their latest hit The Gay Divorcee in which the couple could be seen eating their favorite (no doubt compensated for) lunch. Eddie Cantor sang about ice cream, and his enormously popular film Kid Millions ended with a long song and dance number extolling ice cream. The film made such an impression on one mayor that he declared an "Ice Cream Week." Hollywood stars and ice cream maintained their relationship in decades following the thirties; the broadest and most enduring of these relationships were the Dixie Cup tops.

1938 was the year that Joseph Fleming Greubel started the Valley Dairy chain. He would become (as would his son, Joseph E) an ice cream manufacturer and promoter of international repute.

Then came World War Two. Rationing led to shortages, shortages led to short supply. The appeal of ice cream as the national dessert, however, did not diminish, and not even Mom's Apple Pie caused

Manufacturers and vendors participated in World War II efforts. Dixie incorporated its Hollywood star Dixie Cup top program with military scenes. Bettemen Archive.

greater homesickness among servicemen overseas than did ice cream. War movies produced during the early years of the war were replete with scenes of men who, during breaks in combat, longed for the delights of the soda fountain back in their hometowns.

Rare was the warship that did not have its own facility for making ice cream. Toward the end of the war the navy built a vessel dedicated to the making of ice cream and sent it to the Pacific Theatre. It could produce one gallon of ice cream per second. So powerful was ice cream as an American symbol that the Japanese wartime government took stern measures to have it banned in Japan.

After the war, Americans made up for the wartime shortages. In 1946, American manufacturers produced enough ice cream to provide each citizen of the United States with twenty quarts.

In 1951, the American ice cream industry celebrated its centennial. Jacob Fussell would have been impressed.

Shortly thereafter the great American soda fountains moved toward extinction, to be replaced by such phenomena as embryonic convenience stores to supermarkets. Today, one would be hard pressed to find an authentic soda fountain or the drug store with a magazine rack and soda fountain. The old scoops, milkshake machines, dishes, trays, straw containers, and all those things that made the soda fountain exist in the memories of the older generations - to find them, one must go to antique malls, perhaps flea markets, and, certainly EBay.

Ice cream promoters were quick to use office supplies and post cards to advertise their products. Above is an ink blotter produced in the 1930s by the Horton Company. The post card below suggests that the home ice cream freezer is so simple to operate and child can do it. Courtesy of Ed Marks.

INK BLOTTERS

Courtesy of Ed Marks.

GREETING CARDS & POST CARDS

Courtesy of Ed Marks.

Ice Cream Joe: THE VALLEY DAIRY STORY

TRADE JOURNALS
Courtesy of Ed Marks.

New inventions contributed to the mass production of ice cream.

Top left: The earliest homogenizer, invented by Auguste Gaulin, and patented in 1902.

Center: An early hand-cranked ice cream machine of 1887. Making ice cream in this machine was a tedious process, but a step in the right direction.

Bottom: A steam boiler was combined with a Mills Ice Cream Freezer around 1883.

Ice Cream Joe: THE VALLEY DAIRY STORY

125

NO BOOZE BUT...

Ice Cream Review - April 1933

"With beer soon to be with us once more, what does the future hold for the ice cream manufacturer? Will we have a continuation of conditions such as illustrations above, or will the "gentleman" at the right crowd the ice cream consumer out of the picture?" So says the caption for these illustrations from the Ice Cream Review of April 1933.

It was a toss-up as to which industry would suffer the most after Prohibition - ice cream or soda pop. History proved that neither would suffer. Ice cream sales, especially, grew to monumental proportions.

By themselves, Americans today consume more than two billion gallons of ice cream products per year. Top production states include Pennsylvania, New York, Vermont, California, Texas, and Massachusetts.

Ice Cream Review - April 1933

Ice Cream Joe: THE VALLEY DAIRY STORY

SO DO...
HOLLYWOOD AND BASEBALL AND MUSIC AND THE COMICS AND THE WAR AND THE LADIES

W.C. Fields tastes an ice cream soda, or is it an ice cream and beer soda? Actress Ann Sheridan, pictured on a 1942 Life Magazine cover, enjoys an ice cream soda. Silent screen star Betty Compton, obviously at the beach, clutches her Eskimo Pie. Sixteen-year-old Lana Turner lost in thought while she sips her soda. The scene is from the film They Won't Forget. Lana was discovered, so they say, working at a soda fountain.

Ice Cream Joe: THE VALLEY DAIRY STORY

POPULARITY
~ The Result of Pleasing the Public ~

Flavoring extracts or baseball stars—it's all the same. You get the business when you've got the goods.

That's why hundreds of ice cream manufacturers who have tested scores of vanilla flavors have selected and continue to use

Bowey's Van-Cou
IMITATION VANILLA CONCENTRATE

As a vanilla flavoring, Bowey's Van-Cou deserves its popularity. It contains 62½% of pure vanilla bean extract by volume, and gives a rich, smooth, delightful flavor at an economical cost that will not freeze out.

Babe Ruth, a prodigious gourmand, was a natural to promote any food. The music industry was quick off the mark in promoting ice cream. In this Ice Cream Review Advertisement of 1927, the year he hit sixty home runs, he pays silent testimony to vanilla. He was so well known the advertisers did not need to identify him. As Ed Marks states in his Ice Cream Collectibles: "We are a music loving, ice cream loving society. And with a combination of the two, how could a composer be wrong? Composers have extolled love and romance, the soda fountain, parties, good times, vacations and all the pleasant things we enjoy."

I'LL HAVE VANILLA
Ukulele Accompaniment
Eddie Cantor
M. Witmark & Sons, New York
By Eddie Cantor, Redmond Farrar and Arthur Terker

SHOOT THE SHERBET TO ME, HERBERT!
Words and Music by Ben Homer
Introduced and Featured by Tommy Dorsey

OH! MOTHER I'M WILD
by Howard Johnson, Harry Pease & Eddie Nelson

I SCREAM, YOU SCREAM
WE ALL SCREAM FOR ICE CREAM

Howard Johnson, Billy Moll, Robert King (1927)

In the land of ice and snows
Up among the Eskimos,
There's a college known as Ogiwawa!
You should hear those college boys,
Gee, they make an awful noise
When they sing an Eskimo tra-la-la!

They've got a leader, big cheer leader,
Oh, what a guy!
He's got a frozen face just like an Eskimo Pie!
When he says, "Come on, let's go!"
Though it's forty-five below,
This is what the Eskimos all holler:

Tuesdays, Mondays, we all scream for sundaes,
Sis-boom-bah!
Boola-boola, sarsaparoolla,
If you got chocolate, we'll take vanoola!

I scream, you scream, we all scream for ice cream!
Rah! Rah! Rah!
I scream, you scream, we all scream for ice cream!
Rah! Rah! Rah!
Frosts and malts that are peppered and salted,
Sis-boom-bah!

Oh, spumoni, oh, cartoni,
And confidentially, we'll take baloney,
I scream, you scream, we all scream for ice cream!
Rah! Rah! Rah!
Rah! Rah! Rah! Rah! Rah!

"I Scream, You Scream, We All Scream for Ice Scream" is probably the most famous ice cream song ever written.
People still recite the opening lines today, probably not knowing where it came from.

Ice Cream Joe: THE VALLEY DAIRY STORY

O! MY ESKIMO PIE
(NEW ESKIMO PIE ON A STICK)
Dale Wimbrow (1930) • Radio Commercial (1941)

All the girls are now eating,
All the boys are now treating
New Eskimo Pie
Creamy Pie On A Stick

Go in any direction,
You can buy this confection.
In the heat of summer,
It will cool your day.

In wintertime it helps
To keep the "Doc" away.
It will make you ambitious,
It's so rich and delicious.

There's no bother for mother,
It's good for father and brother,
Little Billy and Mabel!
Eat it all but the label,
And they're sorry they can't eat the stick!

Rich and creamy,
Food for every girl and boy.
You only spend a nickel,
For this bunch of joy.

Buy it, try it, and judge it,
It will balance the budget,
New Eskimo Pie On A Stick.

WORDS AND MUSIC BY
DALE WIMBROW
RADIO'S FAVORITE
SINGING SONG WRITER

"O! My Eskimo Pie" became a famous radio jingle in the 1940s.

SYLVESTER, TWEETY, PORKY, NANCY, SLUGGO, DONALD AMONG OTHERS.

Ice Cream Joe: THE VALLEY DAIRY STORY

Ice cream became an edible morale symbol during World War II. All branches of the military were featured on magazine covers and in ads. Retailers also took the opportunity to ridicule the enemy.

ICE CREAM GOES TO WAR

Ice Cream Joe: THE VALLEY DAIRY STORY

TOPPINGS

Top: Marines freeze ice cream on Bouganville during World War II. Nothing could deny GIs their ice cream, and they would construct freezing apparatus out of whatever material came to hand, from spent shell casings to cast-off aircraft parts.

Bottom: SPARS and Coastguardsmen enjoy ice cream at a soda fountain in Palm Beach, Florida.

Photos: Quartermaster General. United States Coast Guard

During the Civil War, Confederate General Jubal Early organized a covert action into the state of Maryland. His plan was to disrupt Union telegraph lines, and free Confederate prisoners of war. General Bradley Johnson led the 1864 raid with Major Harry Gilmor.

The raid was not as successful as Early had hoped it would be. The two officers, faced with strong Union opposition, turned tail for Virginia. In one of the towns along the way, the raiders discovered an ice cream factory. At the rail station, workers from the factory were loading ice cream into boxcars for delivery to the Union Army.

General Johnson allowed his men, many of them strangers to ice cream, to enjoy the spoils of war. And they did, scooping the delight into anything that would hold it

Ice-makers and refrigerator units were in use in the Navy since 1893. An ice cream maker was installed on the USS Missouri (BB-11) in 1906.

During World War I, a Prussian officer commented, "We have no fear of Americans. They are a nation of ice cream eaters." Though history does not record the effect upon the Doughboys, it is certain that the officer ate the entire crow on his plate. The French, however, capitalized on the American love of ice cream. Despite a severe sugar shortage that would have made the making of ice cream illegal, some Frenchmen opened "blind pigs," or speakeasies. The establishments even had passwords, which the American troops were quick to learn.

The US military brass in World War II ultimately surrendered to the troops' demand for ice cream. The Army Quartermaster General supplied machinery and fixings sufficient enough to produce eighty million gallons of ice cream per year. In 1942-1943, military genius found a way to dehydrate ice cream, and sent 135 million pounds of the stuff to all the theaters of war. All the troops had to do was read the instructions on the label

The word "gedunk" appeared in a 1927 comic strip, and referred to ice cream sundaes. The word became popular in the US Navy, and it meant ice cream and other confections, plus the place onboard ship where the snacks were served. The word is mentioned in Leatherneck Magazine (1937); Robert Joseph Casey's Torpedo Junction 1943); and Robert Olds' Helldiver Squadron (1944).

Ice Cream Joe: THE VALLEY DAIRY STORY

ICE CREAM SODA...
THE LADIES' FAVORITE

Ice Cream Joe: THE VALLEY DAIRY STORY

AN APPEAL TO HEALTH AND "VITALITY"

Saving the Babies By feeding them Ice Cream

My Three Years' Experience with Ice Cream Feeding of Feeble-feeder Infants.

By DR. LUTHER HOWELL

In the earlier decades of the twentieth century there was no question about the health benefits of ice cream. It contributed to "romance," created good appetites among babies, was good for kids, and was a "natural" for breakfast. Bryce Thomson revisited the breakfast idea in the Dairy & Ice Cream Field *(September 1977) issue, where he credits Howard B. Grant with promoting ice cream breakfasts on a grand scale (next page).*

ICE CREAM FOR BREAKFAST — AN IDEA WHOSE TIME HAS COME

(Bryce Thomson (The World's Greatest/Oldest Soda Jerk) is a gifted promoter of ice cream, something he has been doing for many decades to the benefit of colleagues the world over. In September 1977, when he was vice president of Miller Dairy Farms in Eaton Rapids, Michigan, he won the Dairy & Ice Cream Field Idea of the Year. Bryce, in the following article appearing in the September 1977 issue of the trade magazine, extols the virtues of ice cream at breakfast, and credits Howard Grant, then vice president of Dairy & Ice Cream Field, for having marketed the idea on a "grand scale."

We at Miller Dairy Farm have been promoting ice cream breakfasts as far back as the 1940s at Civil Air Patrol "fly-ins." In 1969 we worked with the Chamber of Commerce in sponsoring and Ice Cream Festival in Eaton Rapids.

One morning of the two-day festival was set aside for an ice cream breakfast at our local store. It proved so popular that, three years ago, we started opening three of our ten ice cream parlors for breakfast with ice cream prominently featured on the dairy breakfast menu. Vanilla ice cream on steaming hot oatmeal has been a tradition here at the Miller Farm House breakfast table since 1896.

The Bridgeman-Russell Company of Duluth had tried it commercially as have other ice cream manufacturers. Ice Cream breakfasts gained brief popularity during the Prohibition Era.

Still, I claim, it was Howard B. Grant who first successfully promoted the idea on a grand scale. The year was 1948. Harry Truman was in the White House. In October of that year, the National Ice Cream Retailers were holding their 15th annual convention at the Commodore Hotel in New York City. Howard had accepted the job of heading up local arrangements.

First Howard sold the committee on the ice cream breakfast idea. "The point I was trying to get across is still valid today," he recently told me. "Ice cream is good and good for you any hour of the day or night."

Howard got busy weeks before the breakfast. From New York's Boys' Club, his committee recruited ten-year-old Bobby Cowan and appointed him "Kid Ice Cream for 1948." In the days leading up to the convention, the lad made personal appearances in theatres and on radio and TV talk shows to promote the nutritional aspect of ice cream for breakfast.

Boy Scouts and others competed in a sundae-making contest. "Breakfast of Champions," and "Sunnyside Up," were a couple typical names for the concoctions.

The publicity was enormous. All the major New York papers carried the story. So did the radio and TV stations, and a number of magazines and trade publications.

Walter Winchell mentioned it in his column. Another columnist wrote, "Howard Grant is starting a movement to popularize ice cream for breakfast. So far as ingredients go, his statement 'ice cream for breakfast is a natural,' makes sense to me. It's a form of milk and sugar which, on cereal, are an integral part of the breakfast consumed by a large percentage of the population today."

Other writers were skeptical. One wrote: "From the 'We've Heard Everything Department,' certain segments of the ice cream industry are suggesting to food editors that we propose ice cream as a breakfast food."

It has taken us nearly three decades to wake up to the potential of promoting ice cream for breakfast. Perhaps we shouldn't feel so bad. Only recently did the Florida Citrus Commission come up with their hard-hitting commercial featuring their gal, Anita Bryant. She emphasizes: "Orange juice from Florida — It isn't just for breakfast anymore."

THE GREAT SUNFLOWER SEED CAPER

IDEA OF THE YEAR

VALLEY DAIRY SPROUTS A WORLD'S FIRST

From Dairy and Ice Cream Field
By Joseph E. Greubel

(The trade magazine Dairy and Ice Cream Field honored industry innovators each year with its Idea of the Year trophy. The following comments are from Joe E. Greubel's entry for September 1975).

At the Eastern Regional National Ice Cream Retailers Association meeting in the Fredericksburg, Virginia, I presented some ideas on sales and sales promotion. One of the ideas that really obsessed me was "grow you own flavor." I had seen the surge of popular interest in gardening and that made me eager to dig in on the gardening craze.

I had the idea at the N.I.C.R.A. meeting; I just didn't have the right flavor.

All I could think about was the good promotion ideas: "Look What's Sprouting," "Hoe on Over," and "Lettuce Prove It's True."

Driving back home, I kept coming up with flavors that lacked something special until our store supervisor's wife remarked, "I forget to water Bobby's sunflower."

That hit me like I stepped on a rake and I said, "How about sunflower ice cream?" We headed for the nearest mall to hunt up a health food store and buy some sunflower seeds. At last I had the flavor, and all we talked about on the way home was our newest idea — Sunflower Ice Cream!

Now the problem would be production. I placed a bulk order for toasted and salted sunflowers while we got busy discussing color and flavor. It was the first time we had ever worked with a nut that had an average kernel count of 7,872 to the pound. That gave me the idea, "Our Nuttiest Flavor — Sunflower Ice Cream."

Ice Cream Joe: THE VALLEY DAIRY STORY

We took thousands and thousands of choice sunflower seeds and "planted" them into a sunny yellow and buttery background combined with a secondary color of brown. Then we added whole sunflower seeds to the ice cream through a fruit feeder, in the same manner as we did strawberries and walnuts. Already I could see the sales possibilities.

One of our promotion ideas was a rosette ribbon badge for all our employees. The ribbon colors were the same as the ice cream, and the employees wore it like a sunflower corsage. Since customers liked them so much, and wanted to buy them, we decided to sell them to further promote the product. To do so, we placed color-coordinated point-of-sale signs in brown and yellow in our store windows. In addition, we used flavor strips and table tents. We even made a sign panel for our truck that said, "Look What's Sprouting — Sunflower Ice Cream — Euell Love It." Euell Gibbons was big in the health food trends of the day. We also turned our mailing envelopes into ads by having a low-cost rubber stamp made that said, "Our Nuttiest Flavor — Sunflower Ice Cream," then stamping the envelopes with it.

Some of the major ice cream manufacturers have been advertising "natural flavored" ice creams, but nothing could be as natural as sunflower. In fact, those national ads helped us. We can't help but think that the more they advertise "natural flavors," the more people will go "natural" with our sunflower ice cream.

Our news releases have gained us publicity from front pages to editorial columns. This has all had a tremendous impact on the public, encouraging them to try our new flavor. Promoting a new flavor was and is a lot of fun, and it has not only endeared people to us for being so clever, but it has gotten our employees enthusiastically involved. It has people talking about us, and that's what we wanted to accomplish, along with selling more ice cream.

The new flavor has proven to be more than a flash in the pan. It is now ranked third in flavor sales, and it appeals to both children and adults. The original idea to create a flavor that would appeal to health food faddists is also holding up well. We even have had doctors endorse the health value of sunflower ice cream.

Part of sunflower ice cream's appeal is that people imagine their own flavor when they taste it. Some say that it tastes like a Bit-O-Honey candy bar, while others say it tastes like butter pecan or walnut.

The sunflower processors finally became believers when we reordered seeds after several production runs. They told me that they have set up a special account file on Valley Dairy, and that we opened up a whole new market for their seeds. It just goes to show you that sunflower ice cream is for people, and not just for the birds.

I've gone full circle on the gardening gimmick. I have real sunflowers growing between the shrubs at our ice cream plant. It's just my way to let people know that I'm not kidding when I say we're sprouting a world's first!

Kids love the Sunflower taste!

Greensburg Tribune Review cartoon.

"Would you care to try my sunflower seed sherbet?"

The Greubels receive the 1975 Idea of the Year Award for Sunflower Ice Cream at the Louisville, Kentucky, NICRA Convention. Left to Right: Joe F. Greubel, Joe E. Greubel, Howard B. Grant, Editor of Ice Cream and Dairy Field, Robert Rummel, Valley Dairy.

Ice Cream Joe: THE VALLEY DAIRY STORY

POINT OF SALE AND SPECIAL PROMOS

"I HAD TO EARN JF'S RESPECT"

Virginia Greubel, 2004

Joseph F. Greubel's respect for me did not come easily. I earned it. Even though I had a full-time secretarial job at a local loan and finance company, I worked in the restaurants just to "learn the business." I wasn't the best waitress in the world, nor short-order cook neither, but I certainly went through basic training. I think J.F. thought I was too embarrassed to wait tables, but, truthfully, I didn't have the personality for it. I was not out-going and chatty.

I officially came into the business as an employee in 1987, after I had finished a few classes in graphic arts at the local community college. (I accumulated so many credits over several years, that I finally went and got the degree). I started by designing ads, which was as much fun as it was work. J.F. had always handled the advertising. Some of his ads were pretty "home spun," and I tried to give them a more professional look. One of his ads for chipped ham stated, "Ye, Gods! That's a lot of ham!" Another one read, "Dear Santa, old chap: Would you be so kind as to take a moment out of your busy schedule to do Valley Dairy a favor. Please tell everyone to be sure to pick up their Christmas Ice Cream on or before December 24th. Valley Dairy stores will be closed on Christmas Day. Thanks ever so much, and do have a jolly."

One of his selling points included "china, silverware, and clean restrooms" (I believe this approach was a pre-emptive strike against the newly emerging fast food restaurants). Most of his ads had the "Ice Cream Joe" character's head on them, and it didn't matter whose body the head was on — Santa Claus, the Easter Bunny, whatever! Some of his methods were unique, and effective. He was one of the local pioneers of running ads in the classified (!) section in reverse type. They certainly stood out!

Work was really fun in those times. We were adventurous in creating ice cream flavors and creations. One of the early ones was sunflower ice cream. It happened during the early days of "healthy eating" as promoted by Euell Gibbons. We were fortunate to gain national publicity for the flavor. We also had Sherry Cherry for the United States bicentennial, and CB (coconut bits) when civil band radios were popular. We had the Flaming Cannonball sundae. It was served with a real sparkler.

Everything at Valley Dairy seemed to be done on a shoestring budget. I published a monthly notice that advised our managers of the promotions for the coming months. We didn't have a photocopier, so I had to drive to the Township Office a few blocks from our own, and use the copier to make enough notices for the managers. I couldn't afford to subscribe to a clip art service, so I got old ones from the local newspaper. All the ads at that time were pasted up on a heavy board. I had the local newspaper make veloxes of my originals, and sent them to other papers.

Valley Dairy never had a professionally rendered logo until I began working with a local ad agency.

SENIOR CITIZENS!

VALLEY DAIRY
Family Restaurant Ice Cream Shoppe

helps you enjoy your golden years when you join our

Golden Years Discount Club

The membership is **FREE** and it entitles cardholders aged 60 or over to a 10% DISCOUNT OFF REGULAR MENU PRICES at any Valley Dairy. Not valid on carry-out ice cream or specials.

First, we used a hand-drawn black and white drawing of a Valley Dairy store. Then I did a drawing of western-style lettering that we used for many years. A menu company took these western letters and put them on a curve. This logo was the best looking of all of our efforts. Finally, another agency designed a logo for us, which we have used until just recently.

One of the times that I got a nod of approval from J.F. was when I was still at the community college. I asked him to assist me with a project. The class was assigned to do a TV commercial, and I convinced them to do one on ice cream. I designed the storyboard, and J.F. acted in the ad. It was a good one, and we all enjoyed doing it.

Over the years, Valley Dairy, in promoting and selling its product, went from hand-drawn ads and signs to computer-generated materials, from simple newspaper ads to radio and TV spots to billboards, from four stores to thirteen, and, this year to the World Wide Web.

— You Are Now A Member Of The —

Pier 56 Mini Golf

HOLE - IN - ONE - CLUB

WINDBER, ROUTE 56 EAST
AT FAIRVIEW'S VALLEY DAIRY

Enjoy one free game anytime during the current season.

Mary Jo Greubel with her grandfather, Joe F. Greubel. Boy Scout is Chris Plummer.

Valley Dairy Salutes Scouting

For over 70 years, Scouting has provided opportunities for youth from all segments of American life to develop their potential, make friends and become a vital part of their community.

Valley Dairy and Ice Cream Joe thanks our Boy Scouts for their contribution to our community.

**National Boy Scout Week
Diamond Jubilee
February 3-9**

Ice Cream Joe: THE VALLEY DAIRY STORY

Kid's Day in Latrobe, Pennsylvania, a Chamber of Commerce and Businessmen's promo.

Standing left: Mickey Radman and Joe E. Greubel. They came with a supply of Jo Pops.

Ice Cream Joe: THE VALLEY DAIRY STORY

HERE'S THE SCOOP

AUGUST 1990:
UNIVERSITY OF PITTSBURGH
PITT MAGAZINE

The resume of Joseph E. Greubel (Business '59), if he had one, would read like an entry in the Yellow Pages: "Valley Dairy. Windber, Pennsylvania."

"It sounds odd in today's fast-track world," Greubel, fifty-three, says, "but this is really the only job I've ever wanted or had."

His modest office sits just a few steps from the large, shiny-clean freezer barrels of the manufacturing plant where Valley Dairy ice cream (and, now, frozen yogurt) churns, as it has for more than fifty years.

"I have a very common sense theory when it comes to ice cream ingredients. If it doesn't look and taste good before going into the ice cream, it isn't going to get any better," Joe says.

Such homespun philosophy is spelled out for customers right on the Valley Dairy placemat menus. "My principles have been simple — good food, fair portions, sensible prices, courteous service," writes Joe Greubel senior, still active as chairman of the board at seventy-seven.

A trip to a Valley Dairy still stirs memories of a first date or a Sunday drive for many people in the small towns and suburbs of southwestern Pennsylvania. While some big-city diners try to re-create such nostalgic charm with cleverly appointed décor and wise-cracking waitresses, Greubel knows he's got the real thing: triple-dip malted milk shakes and hot meat loaf platters.

When the company president walks in to the Richland shopping-center store and takes a booth, nobody seems particularly impressed. Lisa, the waitress, calmly pours the boss's coffee while joking with him about not getting enough sleep. A couple of the regulars interrupt their afternoon town meeting to ask, not so gently, "Where have you been?"

"I think it does us both good," Greubel says of his close ties with the staff. "It's good for their morale, and it's good for my morale." It's not unusual, he adds, for an employee to move from dishwasher to store manager and then off to college or a successful career. "I like to call this the "Valley Dairy Academy."

On the other side of the counter, Greubel knows that what Valley Dairy offers customers is more than a meal. "Someone might say we are in the food business," he says, "but, really, we're in the people business. The types of pleasure we sell are simple pleasures. It's not all that expensive to treat yourself to the best ice cream, or to a hot lunch. It's the kind of extravagance that everyone can afford."

The desire to break new ground has been handed down to Joe Greubel along with the years of business savvy. "Some people are in business to make money," he says. "For me, my thrill comes from coming up with a new idea and making it work."

One idea that won Greubel industry recognition was the sunflower seed ice cream that he created in 1975. He also launched what he believes is the first-ever ice cream "white sale." He says, "I figured that if it worked for pillowcases and sheets, why not ice cream?" So, each year, during the "white sale," Valley Dairy gives a half-price half-gallon of vanilla with the purchase of any other half-gallon.

"Dad started this company in the middle of the Depression, and if you were raised in business in that era, you learned to do anything and everything to survive," says Greubel. "Sometimes that meant that rather than getting the job I was most qualified for, I got the most recent vacancy."

"We would love to grow, but not too big," says Greubel. "I never want to get so big that we decide to no longer use real cherries in the cherry-vanilla ice cream."

Ice Cream Joe: THE VALLEY DAIRY STORY

THE VALLEY DAIRY RADIO JINGLE

For breakfast, lunch or dinner,
Be sure to pick a winner,
Valley Dairy Restaurants

Banana splits and more,
Ice cream you'll adore,
Valley Dairy Restaurants

Anytime's the time,
Delicious meals,
Terrific deals,
That's what you'll find,
Valley Dairy's just for you.

There's Ice Cream Joe
To welcome you,
Your family too.
So good, so right,
Ice cream tonight.

For breakfast, lunch or dinner,
Be sure to pick a winner,
Valley Dairy Restaurants,
Your favorite restaurant.

Ice Cream Joe: THE VALLEY DAIRY STORY

FOR THE LAPELS

Buttons produced by the G.P. Grundlach Company of Cincinnati, Ohio.
Ribbons for Valley Dairy produced by the Stineman Ribbon Company.

Ice Cream Joe: THE VALLEY DAIRY STORY

FOR THE TABLES...

... POINT OF SALE

WITH A LITTLE HELP FROM OUR FRIENDS

From the beginning, ice cream manufacturers and retailers were courted and assisted by numerous ancillary industries, whose ads appeared (and continue to appear) in various trade magazines, notably *The Ice Cream Review*, *The Dairy and Ice Cream Field*, and the *National Dipper*. The selections which follow are gleaned from trade journals, past and present.

The Biggest Thing You Can Do For Your Retailer

is to make it possible for him to dispense your Ice Creams, Sherbets, and other frozen products—to a larger and better satisfied public — through a Valerius-Built ICE-O-MATIC Soda Fountain!

Isn't your present greatest problem to have your delicious products delivered to the consumer in as clean, sanitary and wholesome condition as they are when you deliver them to the retailer?

And is that possible with any salt-and-ice system, or with any application that is not built to meet the demands of these days of snappy merchandising? It is not.

We are on the threshold of a wonder Ice Cream era. To meet the growing public demand for your goods, ... must be the finest possible me... dispensing.

Naturally the retailer looks ... manufacturer, for guidance ... of re-selling your product... believe the best service ... such a retailer is to m... him to get, through y... Fountain. Every ... your goods thro... will make more ... therefore, for ... strated beyon...

Let us send you complete details regarding t... remarkably efficient applicatio...

VALERIUS REFRIGERATION
456 Jefferson Street

This Ice-O-Matic is equipped with the famous Niser unit. It is the last word in efficiency.

A 40-Car trainload of Nickels for DIXIES

5¢

That is the price the American people paid the ice cream industry for Dixies during the past 12 months.

Forty Carloads of Nickels!
Each month bigger and better than the one before.

DIXIES

Ice Cream Joe: THE VALLEY DAIRY STORY

Geo. F. Jones Company
will be at Cleveland Convention in
Booth 2W-11
down main stairway — forward to the right

Illuminated Displays with **Reproductions of Ice Cream in Glass**

Our list of completely satisfied Ice Cream Companies is steadily growing,—making necessary the purchase of the factory property herewith shown, in order that we can better serve the Ice Cream Industry.

Be sure to see this beautiful booth! 2W-11
down main stairway — forward to the right

GEO. F. JONES COMPANY, Box 298, JEANNETTE, PA.

NOW is the time
to gather those *Roadside Dollars* with this new stand—

Shaped like an Eskimo's IGLOO
Patent Pending

THERE are many logical sites in your community for this new Roadside Stand. It is neat, attractive, and sales-compelling and will gather in many roadside dollars which you can get in no other manner. This Roadside Stand is unusual in shape and soon becomes a landmark, a showpoint, a meeting place—genuine, sales-producing advertising. It is shaped like an Eskimo's Igloo, made of sheet metal, has six windows and a full-length serving counter on the inside. Shipped knock-down with all necessary bolts and braces. Write for prices now.

The FAUNCE & FAUNCE Co.
1609 Washington Street
TOLEDO, OHIO

Patent Pending

"The BIG CONE"   "The BIG CONE"

"It tells them what you have to sell"
Every "Big Cone" owner is a first class dealer for you.

Steel Building 16' dia. x 30' high
WEIGHT 3000 lbs.—COMPLETE—READY TO ERECT
WITHOUT SOLDER—PORTABLE

"The BIG CONE"

A real Ice Cream "Specialty Store Building." Wonderful sales records furnished by users; also letters from reputable ice cream manufacturers who know about the Big Cone gallonage, copies furnished.
Remove temptation from competitors by ordering NOW.
60 day option for county with purchase of one building.

Choose Your Dealers

LEROY CORLISS
NATIONAL SALES AGENT
ALHAMBRA - CALIFORNIA
Manufacturing Plant—Glendale, California

Ice Cream Joe: THE VALLEY DAIRY STORY

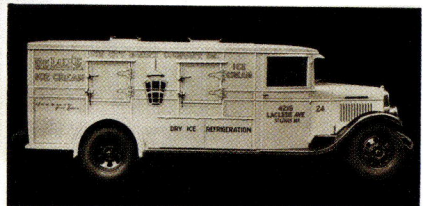

Ice Cream Joe: THE VALLEY DAIRY STORY

Why Not Sell A *Brick* of Water Ice?

A NEW idea!—Orange, Raspberry, Pineapple—three delicious water ices moulded in Neapolitan brick form—Just like ice cream! Yesterday you could never make a water ice brick because yesterday's water ices would "water down", become streaky, syrupy—could not be packed and repacked until sold.

Today—with TEXTOR—it's a different story. Marvelously smooth, homogenous water ices. Scratchy icy crystals banished. A better-looking, evenly flavored, readily salable product that will build new business for you.

What TEXTOR Will Do for You:
1—TEXTOR makes possible water ices in brick form.
2—TEXTOR prevents the formation of icy crystals.
3—TEXTOR eliminates streaking and "watering down"
4—TEXTOR-made ices give added lustre to fancy forms and moulds.

Get your share of the profits made possible by using TEXTOR. Judge for yourself the many advantages of this odorless, colorless, tasteless stabilizer for water ices. A free sample will be sent on request. Write for it TODAY

Gumpert's Textor

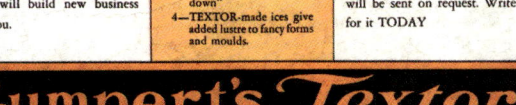

A Product of S. Gumpert Co., Inc. Brooklyn, N.Y.

« « PROUD to be a Member of the Eskimo Pie Family » »

ESKIMO PIE

If you have a sales or distribution problem — If you want to increase sales and build good will, write us for a Mohican Balloon Plan to fit your business. SAMPLES and PRICES GLADLY FURNISHED

FOR THE PAST 6 YEARS
Suppliers of
Mohican Advertising Balloons
TO THE
ESKIMO PIE CORPORATION

THE MOHICAN RUBBER CO., ASHLAND, OHIO

« « PROUD to be a Member of the Eskimo Pie Family » »

POPSICLES

PATENTS NO. 1,470,524 - 1,505,592 - 1,563,121 - 1,718,997 - 1,734,765 - OTHER PATENTS PENDING

POPSICLE CORPORATION OF THE UNITED STATES
1819 BROADWAY --- NEW YORK, U.S.A.

REPRESENTED BY TWO EXCLUSIVE AGENTS

JOE LOWE CORPORATION
BUSH TERMINAL BLDG. No. 8
BROOKLYN, N.Y.

CITRUS PRODUCTS COMPANY
11 EAST AUSTIN AVENUE
CHICAGO, ILL.

Introducing CREAMSICLE

TRADE MARK REG. U.S. PAT. OFF.

A NEW STICK CONFECTION

Your Ice Cream Bar Coated with delicious Fruit or Chocolate Fudge Flavor

The HIT of the SHOW

See It! Taste It!
BOOTH 34 A
New Orleans Convention Auditorium
JOE LOWE CORPORATION
NEW YORK

Ice Cream Joe: THE VALLEY DAIRY STORY

Ice Cream Joe: THE VALLEY DAIRY STORY

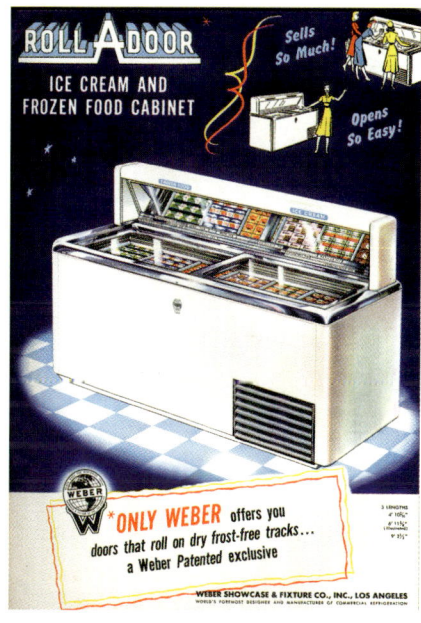

Ice Cream Joe: THE VALLEY DAIRY STORY

Ice Cream Joe: THE VALLEY DAIRY STORY

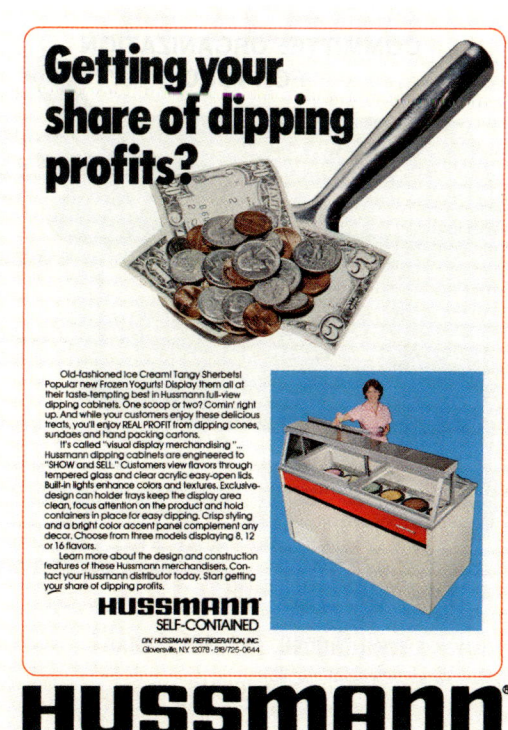

Ice Cream Joe: THE VALLEY DAIRY STORY

TOPPINGS
FROM THE ICE CREAM REVIEW

December 1933 — "Notice." Anyone knowing the whereabouts of Henry S. Jones, formerly a salesman calling on ice cream manufacturers, will please correspond with his wife, Mrs. Jones, 500 Washington Avenue, Houston, Texas. [Editor's note: The names and address have been changed to protect the innocent].

October 1928 — "Big Fire Sale Saturday." Owing to the extreme hot weather we are obliged to carry on this sale. Now the ice cream wasn't damaged by the fire we had, but will be by the weather if we don't sell it. Sale starts at 4:30 P.M. as the Midget Ice Cream Factory, St. Mary's, Ohio.

October 1928 — "African Gold Coast Has First Soda Fountain." In Accra, Gold Coast, [Ghana], has Africa's first soda fountain. American style ice cream sodas and sundaes seem to be finding favor with the inhabitants of that city.

February 1930 — "Ralph Waldo Emerson Sets Record." South Dakota's malted milk king is Ralph Waldo Emerson, University of South Dakota football star who won his title by drinking five double-thick full pint malteds in five minutes, and, for good measure, drank four more in less than another five minutes.

February 1930 — "Pittsburgh to Spend $10 Million for Cones." Approximately $10 million will be spent for ice cream cones in Pittsburgh, PA, in 1930, estimates the statistician for the Pittsburgh C of C. These cones, if placed end to end, would reach from coast to coast.

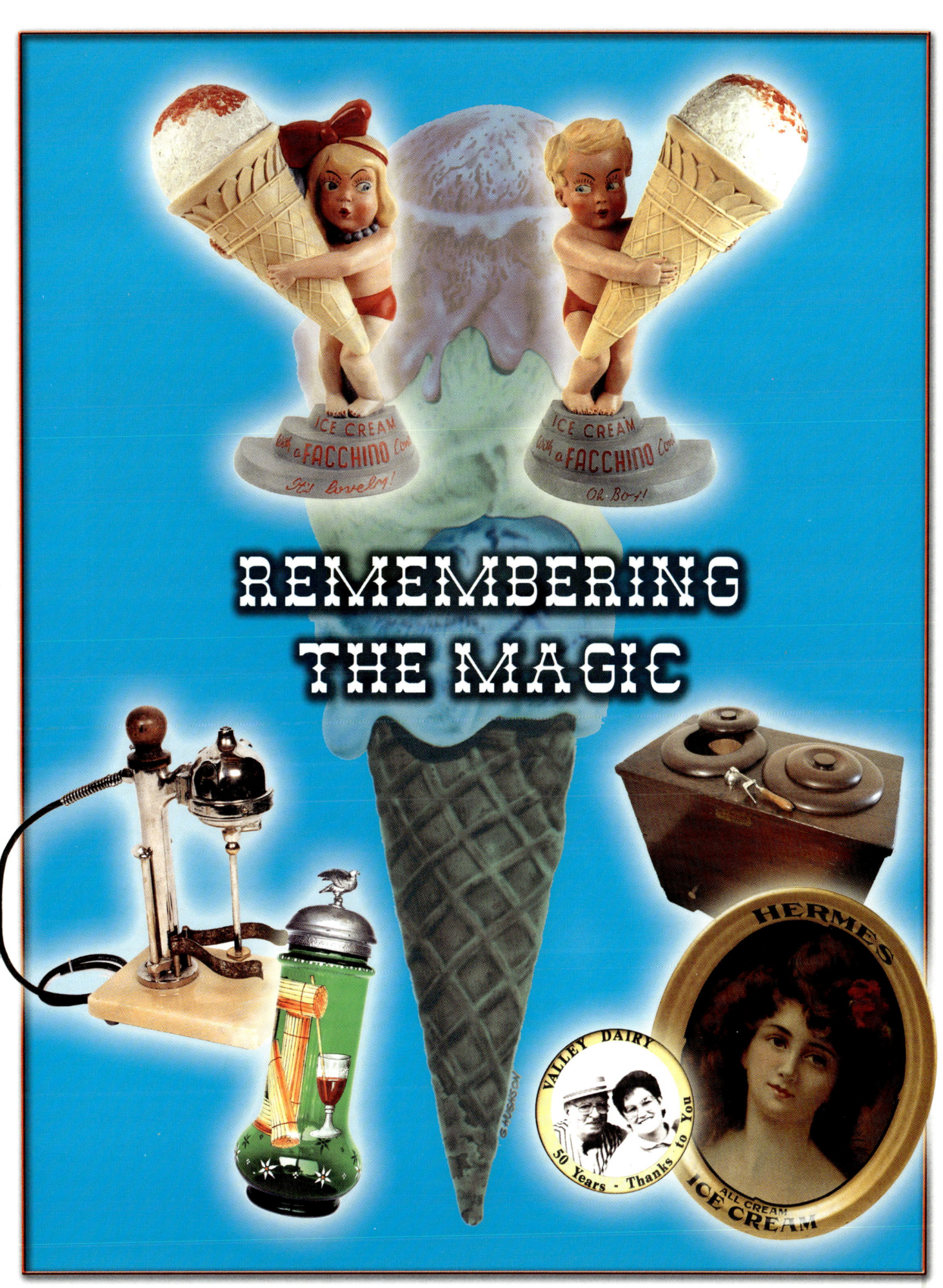

THE WAY IT WAS

What is America's favorite treat? What is America's favorite dessert? If you asked these questions of a thousand people, it wouldn't be surprising if nine-hundred-and-ninety-nine of them answered, "Ice cream!" Neither would it be surprising if much of the world would answer the same.

Yet, despite its centuries-old origins in Europe, ice cream, like the short story, has become a special American institution, along with the corner drug store soda fountain, the soda jerk, the soda, the milkshake, the sundae, and the banana split, all of which have been preserved in American popular culture through Hollywood cartoons and films. Who will ever forget such classics as Bugs Bunny the Good Humor Man defeating Japanese troops with hand grenade-laced ice cream bars on a Pacific Island in World War II, or the small-town soda fountain as a primary setting in scores of family-oriented movies, and as a motif in the fox-hole conversations of combat infantrymen in dozens of war films. Music, toys, office products, trade cards, greeting cards, old-time glassware like banana split dishes, penny licks, straw holders, plus fountain accoutrements like antique dippers, hand freezers, milk shake machines, serving trays, point-of-sale posters, and a host of other memorabilia, though common back when, today are widely sought after as collectibles, not only for their monetary value, but also for the nostalgia they can evoke in the minds of those who still remember.

Sooner or later, the ice cream collectibles "industry" had to produce its first unofficial historian. This was Ed Marks, a Lititz, Pennsylvania, resident who had earned a degree in Dairy Manufacturing from Colorado State University, and went on to a long career in the ice cream industry. In 1958, he created the ice cream and soda fountain operations for the American Pavilion at the Brussels World Fair in Belgium, where he also took the opportunity to introduce to Europe the first soft-serve ice cream.

In 1975, Ed wrote a magazine article on the history of ice cream. His research into the subject got him interested in ice cream memorabilia. In 1982, Ed founded The Ice Screamers, a collector's organization for ice cream parlor and soda fountain memorabilia collectors. Ed edited the organization's newsletter The Ice Screamer until 2003, when he turned that duty over to Thor and Patty Foss of Ephrata, Pennsylvania. Today, The Ice Screamers number over 800 members.

Ed Marks

Perhaps the most sought after collectibles are scoops and dippers. For decades, ice cream had been spooned into serving dishes, a process that Clewell considered to be inefficient. Then, on May 3, 1878, William Clewell, a confectioner from Reading, Pennsylvania, received a patent for his "ice cream disher." He took his patented idea to Valentine Clad, a Philadelphia tinsmith, who fashioned the disher, a conical mold with a key-operated scraper that released the ice cream onto a dish. The same basic type is still in use. For some mysterious reason, an inordinate number of subsequent patents for different kinds of dippers originated in western Pennsylvania.

In his book *Ice Cream Collectibles*, Ed Marks describes the most common types of collectible dippers:

> Ice cream dippers/scoops differ from each other in three regards. The first is the shape of the portion, which can be round, conical, or a flat slab. The second distinction is to be found in the size of the portion. Generally, on the scraper blade inside the dipper you

CLAD'S ICE CREAM DISHERS.

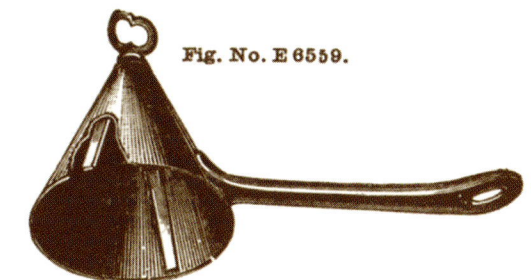

With Seamless Stamped Bowl.

The Bettmann Archive

will find a number that indicates the number of portions that particular scoop will yield from a one-quart container. The numbers run as follows: 6, 8, 10, 12, 16, 20, 40. The smaller the number, the larger the portion. This sort of dipper was introduced by Raymond B. Gilchrist in 1914. In general, the largest and the smallest are those that are in greatest demand with collectors. The third distinction among dippers/scoops lies with what is called the release mechanism. This refers to the method used to get the ice cream out and onto the plate or ice cream cone. The early ones had a turnkey. Some have a squeeze handle, while the majority have a thumb lever, which causes the action.

Numerous patents for dippers were issued for a couple of decades after Clewell obtained his; all of them needed two hands to operate, one hand to hold the handle, and the other to turn the key. Perhaps the earliest "one handed" scoop was E.C. Baughman's 1894 model. Baughman's invention made it easier on the soda jerk, who could release the ice cream by squeezing a handle with one hand, while using the other to hold the dish.

Popular in England and the Continent in the nineteenth century to about the mid-nineteen twenties were the "penny licks," small glasses filled with ice cream that the buyer licked out, then returned the glass to the vendor. It was rare for the penny lick to be washed before another person used it. Health authorities eventually deemed that penny licks were the cause of communicable diseases, especially TB, and they were outlawed.

Eighteenth-century French nobles eat ice cream from "penny dreadfuls."

Ice Cream Joe: THE VALLEY DAIRY STORY

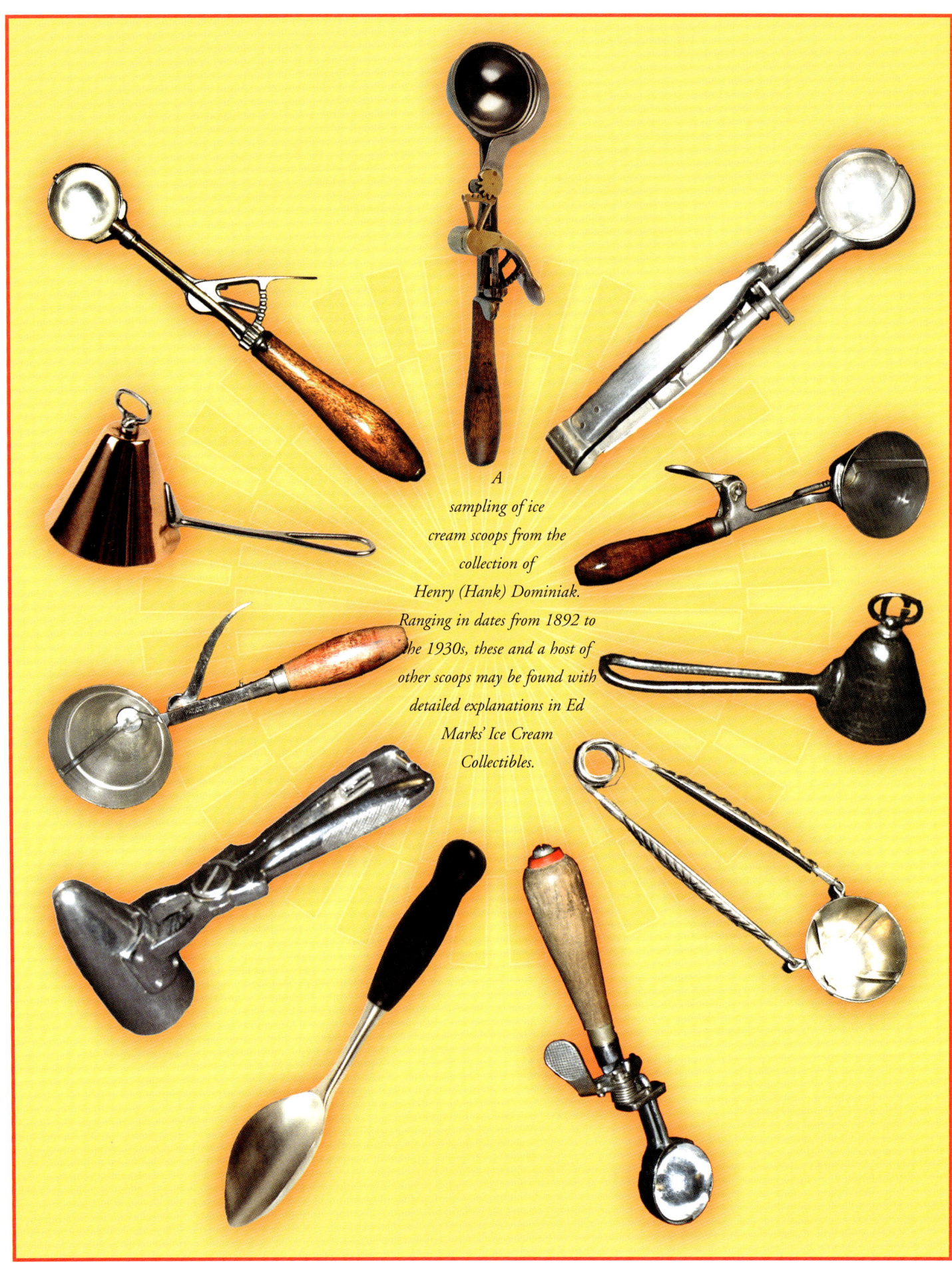

A sampling of ice cream scoops from the collection of Henry (Hank) Dominiak. Ranging in dates from 1892 to the 1930s, these and a host of other scoops may be found with detailed explanations in Ed Marks' Ice Cream Collectibles.

Ice Cream Joe: THE VALLEY DAIRY STORY

A collage of popular ice cream collectibles. Kewpie dolls, celebrity cartons, trays, molds, music sheets, children's books, and a toy vending cart.

Ice Cream Joe: THE VALLEY DAIRY STORY

The Ice Cream Review, one of the industry's renowned trade journals, now defunct, served the industry for decades. Joe E. Greubel was fortunate enough to obtain an almost complete set through the 1960s. The journals, with their colorful colors, were filled with historical articles, marketing strategies, humorous columns, convention notices, and advertisements. The cover for January 1929 was somewhat optimistic, considering that October of that year marked the beginning of the Great Depression.

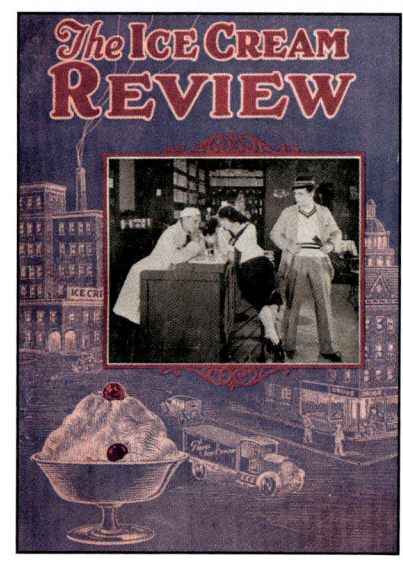

Ice Cream Joe: THE VALLEY DAIRY STORY

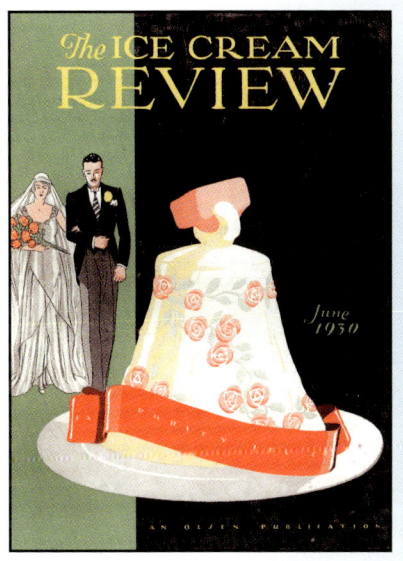

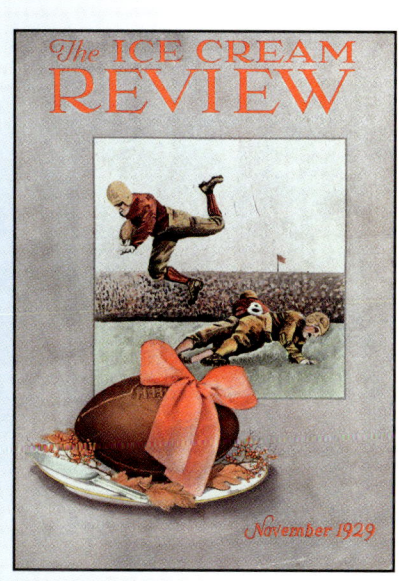

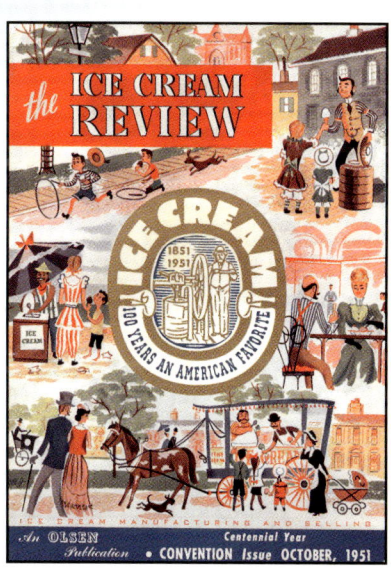

Ice Cream Joe: THE VALLEY DAIRY STORY

The milkshake machine (above left) of the 1940s is recognizable even today. The hand-operated contraption (bottom left) probably must have been something to behold as it mixed milkshakes. It probably served equally well for martinis.

Today's strawholders pale considerably when compared to the Victorian marvels on the right.

Ice Cream Joe: THE VALLEY DAIRY STORY

Items from the Greubel collection. Most interesting is the two container ice box that was used in pre-refrigeration days.

Ice Cream Joe: THE VALLEY DAIRY STORY

TOPPINGS

In the 1960s, Rose Catanzano-Pascal, today Sales Manager at the Holiday Inn, Pittsburgh International Airport, sang the following song that was specially composed for a musical performed at Swissvale High School.

Ice Cream Joe

I call him Ice Cream Joe.
He is the most delicious boy I know.
Every time I kiss him him I feel mighty fine.
He kisses 33 flavors.

Pineapple, peach, coconut, and banana,
Some of each chocolate too.
I tell you when we kiss,
He kisses 33 flavors.

I want the world to know,
How much I love my little Ice Cream Joe.

He kisses 33 flavors.

JIM NORRIS
About Joe Greubel
[Sent to the editors, March 3, 2004]

Jim Norris
Past President NICRA

It's been seventeen years since I last saw Joe E. Greubel, but we do communicate now and then. Back when I was active in NICRA, Joe and I used to consider us competitors in the "Idea of the Year Contest." I think I won it three times. I don't know how many times Joe may have won. I do recall his winning once with Sunflower Ice Cream. Can you believe that? I'm sure he used some sort of skullduggery to pull that off. Now he's competing against Harry Gentry from Texas, and I don't think he's doing so good!

In 1958 I went to work for Ehrler's Dairy as a home delivery milkman. I spent fourteen years in this capacity, and, in 1972, I was made a route supervisor. In 1973 I moved to the store division as manager. At that time, we had six dairy stores, with a seventh under construction. The stores carried a complete line of dairy products, as well as packaged ice cream. A full fountain was an integral part of each location.

A dairy cooperative bought out the private company in 1977. The existing stores were quite profitable, so the co-op expanded to twenty-two stores. By that time, peoples' buying habits were changing, and only a few of the stores turned a profit. I retired in 1993. One year later, the co-op stores were defunct. A new owner had taken over the day after I retired, and it seems he took all the cash to bail out a troubled operation in another state. He went to jail for some kind of violation of Federal law.

In the Louisville area, where I live, the name "Ehrler's" is still to be found associated with ice cream. A former store supervisor was able to get the rights for the name from the co-op. The name is used only at concession stands located at all the major sporting, entertainment, and display shows in the city. For a low-budget operation, it is very successful.

Now that I'm retired, I have no connection with ice cream other than for my morning coffee break at the local Dairy Queen. I spend my free time hunting for wild turkey and fishing for anything that swims. I spend the rest of my time doing artwork in wood.

Valley Dairy lives on, but Ehrler's Dairy, as we knew it, is history.

THE EHRLER'S JINGLE:

When do you go on a Special Kind of Day,
When you want to treat the family in a special kind of way?
Well, it's no big problem, 'cause it's right on your way,
And the name of the place is Ehrler's.

Strawberry cones and chocolate shakes,
All the good things Ehrler's makes,
They always know just what it takes,
To make things great at Ehrler's.

Ehrler's, gonna get a double dip,
Ehrler's, maybe a banana split.
Tastes like heave in a sugar cone,
Daddy, please, can we take some home.

So. Where do you go when you want a treat?
Something Yummy we can eat.
We know a place that can't be beat,
And the name of the place is… name of the place is..
Name of the place is…
EHRLER'S

THE NORRIS WOODCUT

January 17, 2001

Dear Joe:

How's things going? I have been very negligent in keeping in touch. I thought maybe if I made a peace offering, you might forgive me, but I doubt it. Oh, well! So much for friendship made many years ago. I know you can't do the things that I do (like going the club (Dairy Queen) every day for coffee. You have got to realize, my friend, that I am now seventy years old, and I can't follow you through the streets of Boston (like a maniac) the way we did some twenty years ago (but I still miss it — the way we were back then).

The enclosed piece is my version of part of your logo. I say "version" because all I had to go on was the return address on your envelope. This is an artist's piece, and, being a woodworking artist, I did it the same way. The details are not that accurate, but I hope you like it.

In case you are interested in how many pieces of wood there are in the work, I will tell you, just in case you want to run one of your classic promo contests with your employees or customers. The number is 3,823. That's a lie. I made that up to confuse you. That's my old address on Peachtree Avenue.

The real number of wood pieces is 156.

Jim

Ice Cream Joe: THE VALLEY DAIRY STORY

Ice Cream People helping Ice Cream People since 1933.

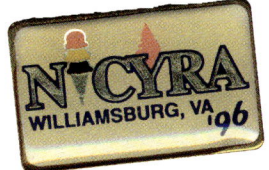

The National Ice Cream Retailers Association is a trade organization whose members are in the retail ice cream and frozen dessert business. Its members are located all across the United States, Canada and several other countries. Since 1933 NICRA has helped hundreds of ice cream and frozen dessert entrepreneurs get started and prosper.

NICRA sponsors the annual Bryce Thomson Scholarship Fund for full-time or part-time employees of active members. It also holds an annual covention in major cities, and publishes a yearbook and a monthly bulletin which inserts Bryce Thomson's popular "Sundae School Newsletter."

Ice Cream Joe: THE VALLEY DAIRY STORY

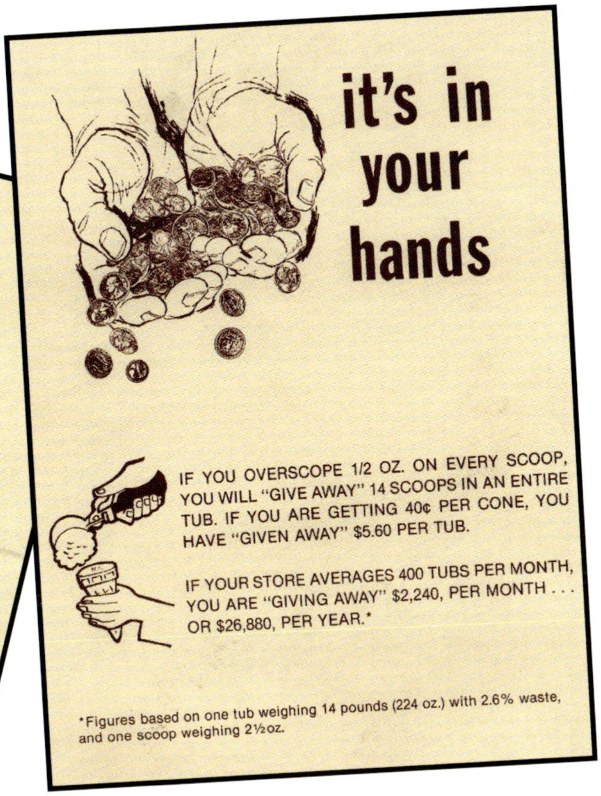

Bottom left to top right: Three promotional pieces prepared by Virginia Greubel for NICRA. Bottom right: Caricature of Melissa "Missy" Greubel done at the NICRA convention in Oklahoma City.

Ice Cream Joe: THE VALLEY DAIRY STORY

NASHVILLE'S ANSWER TO AMERICAN IDOL

The NICRA Talent Show, Nashville, Tennessee, 1984. Left to right: Mary Jo Greubel, age nine, Tom Anderson, President of Colonial Ice Cream, St. Charles Illinois, Chris Anderson, Melissa Greubel, age 13.

Joe E. Greubel on stage at the NICRA Nashville, Tennessee, convention, 1984. Torn between the microphone and the . . . .!

Cowboy Joe E. Greubel as he appeared to an artist at the NICRA Oklahoma City convention.

Ice Cream Joe: THE VALLEY DAIRY STORY

JOE E. GREUBEL'S
BANQUET ADDRESS AT THE NICRA
CONVENTION, 1983

NICRA AFTER FIFTY YEARS
1933-1983

. . . . Instead of looking backward, I considered looking ahead into our next fifty years.

The ice cream business has become such an "in business" that more and more people will be turning to us as one of the "Get-Rich-Quick" business of the future. Even Pillsbury thinks getting into the ice cream business will put them in the dough! Ice cream is perceived by most everyone as a terrific product, and we have flavors to please everyone. Ice cream is rich in tradition. It is festive, wholesome, nutritious, highly convenient, delicious, and versatile. It is as good or better than ever. The ice cream business is on a roll, heading for the year 2033.

We've always been light years ahead with our edible container, the cone! The computer chip will not replace chocolate chip, but computers and electronic technology will show up in more than our cash registers. Computers will be making an impact upon every business, and ours will be no exception.

Perhaps the talking cabinet is just down the road. The dip case, programmed to suggest today's feature flavor, could be welcoming customers to your store, suggesting the day's featured flavor. It might even provide ingredient information for those who would like to know.

Video menu units at your booth or counter could display fountain ice cream creations. Customers could push buttons to create their own a la carte specials. Equipped with a printer, the unit could even provide a guest check to the customer — that is if we are still using checks in 2033. If not, the machine will accept your bank card. By this time the country will be well into the cashless society.

The digital dipper will be a hands-on tool. It will show portion, weight, and yield per container. Controls will be tighter as a result. The digital dipper might even be electronically sensitized to detect any foreign object, something insurance companies will probably require as liability rates keep soaring.

Robots will be of major importance to our business. They will have become the new major home appliance. Shorter work weeks and robots to help at home with domestic duties, will give people more time to dine out and treat themselves. Flexible retirement age and increased life spans will make the senior citizens a major part of our population. Even now, our lessening emphasis on youth will in the future turn us even more to catering to an older population.

According to Changing Times Magazine, by 2017 we will be paying $5.33 for a pound of butter, $6.47 for a gallon of gasoline, $1.34 for a first-class stamp, and $52,186 for a four-door Chevrolet. Just think where the double-dip cone and the half-gallon will be! If you think you will have trouble affording these things, cheer up. If, during the next thirty-five years, consumer prices rise at the same rate as they did in the past thirty-five years, the median annual family income could increase to $165,671, up from $22,388 in 1982.

A study by Frost and Sullivan reported that the market for process dairy items will build from $8.3 billion in 1981 to $12 billion by 1990. As ice cream manufacturers and retailers, we have to promote our product to ensure our share of that increase. And we have an advantage as we consider our competitive edge into the next century — our ability to provide the "human touch."

As we move toward a society filled with computers, robots, and other high-tech items, the more people will look for a counter-balancing human response. Customers will be starved for service. Profit may be the bottom line, but people are the top line. At our 1980 convention in Gettysburg, Pennsylvania, Wayne Thede said it all when he stated, "We are in the people business!"

Having a feel for business still requires a personal touch, with both employees and customers. Even with digital watches that perform multi-functions, people still want a human voice to tell them what time it is.

For years, Don was a salesman for Eat It All Ice Cream Cones in Western Pennsylvania, and a friend of Valley Dairy. Now retired, he resides in Chalk Hill, Pennsylvania. There really was a Gray's Lake Ice Cream Factory

DON FLOWERS
WHAT IS GRAY'S LAKE FAMOUS FOR... A TRUE STORY, OR FRACTURED HISTORY?

The town of Grayslake, Illinois, lay between a third lake and a fourth lake. This presented a problem. Besides not being able to spell, the townsfolk shied away from calling the town first or second lake or even fifth lake. They stuck with another name. They weren't good with math either.

Well, there was an old machine-gun target range (which was franchised by Public Enemy Machine Gun Kelly near the company. One day Al Capone and his buddies came out to practice and stopped at the Grays Lake Ice Cream Company. Al had a tooth problem and asked the soda jerk to put some milk in with the ice cream. The fellow did, and shook it up. That's when milkshakes got their name.

On the way back to Chicago, Al's group ran into Evangelist Billy Sunday. They told him how good the ice cream was at the Grays Lake Ice Cream Company. Not too much later, Sunday went out to try some. He wanted it in a dish. The soda jerk asked, "Do you want chocolate on this, Sunday?"

The soda jerk couldn't spell "Sunday," so he spelled it phonetically. But from that time on, it stuck, and that's how we got "Sundae." The Reverend decided to have ice cream socials at his gatherings. Forever after, ice cream socials were accepted as a church event on Sundays, thanks to the soda jerk at Grays Landing.

Now we go to the sad part of the story. Grays Lake Ice Cream Company received most of its milk and cream from the famous O'Leary Barn in Chicago. One day a cow kicked over a kerosene lantern and, ergo. The Big Chicago Fire. Now, with no more cream or milk, Grays Lake Ice Cream Company had to close.

Can you imagine Mayor Daley's predicament? He has to tell Big Al that there is not a drop of ice cream left to make milk shakes. So what does Big Al do? He goes into the production of spirits. Wow? He tells Reverend Sunday to go buy some bananas and split them and dream of ice cream. An angel appears to Billy and tells him how to make banana splits. So we do owe a debt of gratitude to Grayslake for being there, even it they can't spell, or count.

Al Capone almost made the Grays Lake Ice Cream Company very well known. He took an empty pint of Grays Lake ice cream, and had his chauffeur send it to Andy Warhol in Smock, Pennsylvania, for him to draw a picture of it so that he could display it in his living room. One day, the chauffeur was taking out the garbage on his way to the Post Office, and got mixed up. He tossed the ice cream container and mailed a Campbell's soup container instead. Too bad for the Grays Lake Ice Cream Company. Great for Campbell's Soup.

So now we know what Grayslake is famous for.

But one more thing. Public Enemy Number One, John Dillinger, had a date one evening with a very famous lady. He got a craving for a big chocolate Sunday with lots of red cherries on top. He planned to take the lady out to the Grays Lake Ice Cream Company for the treat. She said (shyly or slyly) that she would wear a real nice red outfit that would complement the cherries on the ice cream sundae.

But when John went to pick her up, she told him she had a headache, and could they go to the movies in downtown Chicago, and she would buy him a big bag of popcorn. Reluctantly, he agreed, even though he loved ice cream more than popcorn. Coming out of the movies, the lady walked a little ahead of John, and the FBI shot him. She really tricked him. It was a set-up. Moral: Don't eat popcorn. Eat ice cream instead.

Mr. and Mrs. Don Flowers at an Ice Screamers' convention.

LYNDA UTTERBACK AND "THE NATIONAL DIPPER"

Fifteenth Anniversary Issue

Lynda Utterback has a Bachelor Degree in Journalism from Mundelein College, which is part of Loyola University in Chicago, Illinois.

Lynda has worked in the publishing industry for more years than she cares to admit, always working on trade publications geared to the retail market.

In 1982 she joined Transworld Exhibits, Inc., as head of their publishing department and charged with the responsibility of producing two trade publications and expanding the publishing department.

In 1984, she found herself in the ice cream store of a high school friend, eating an ice cream cone. When she asked her friend if there was a magazine for ice cream stores, the answer was no. The idea for *The National Dipper* was born.

After spending a year researching the market and a summer working evenings in her friend's ice cream store, Lynda presented the idea to her publisher and in April 1985 the first issue of *The National Dipper* was published.

In December 1992, Lynda purchased the magazine from Transworld Exhibits and became the publisher/editor.

She is also owner and president of JLM Unlimited, Inc., which produces point of sale and training materials for ice cream stores and the Executive Director of the National Ice Cream Retailers Association.

THE ICE SCREAMER

Recapturing the Fun and Magic of Those
Wonderful Olde Ice Cream Parlour-Soda Fountain Days

Issue #100   Established 1982   November 2003

Right: Patty and Thor Foss, current editors of The Ice Screamer, a definitive magazine for collectors of ice cream memorabilia. The magazine was founded by Ed Marks. The group, Ice Screamers, boasts a growing membership that presently stands at over 700.

Ice Cream Joe: THE VALLEY DAIRY STORY

YESTERDAY'S PRICES

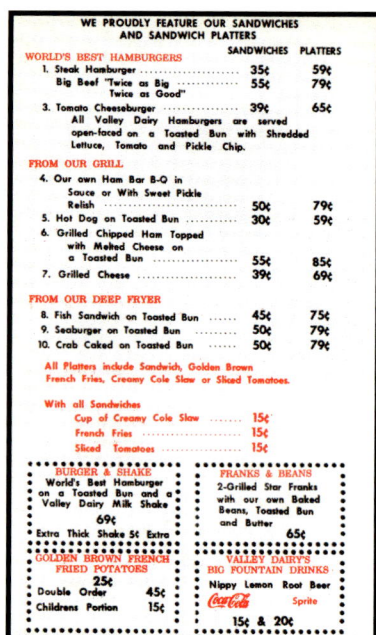

WHAT EVERY SODA JERK NEEDS TO KNOW

Dipping Tips

TRAINING AND PRACTICE: KEYS TO UNIFORM PORTIONS

Opinions on the proper method of dipping ice cream vary within the industry. But illustrated here are the time-tested techniques recommended by the majority of experienced ice cream people, who also concur that portion control can only be achieved through a training program that is continuous and involves plenty of practice. Don't be influenced by industry charts which show, for example, that a No. 24 dipper will produce a portion of ice cream averaging 1 5/8 ounces by weight. Experience shows that a No. 24 dipper can be used to roll ice cream into a ball which may vary in weight from 1 1/2 to 5 ounces -- depending on who' doing the dipping! This is why management must establish a rigid rule on the size of the dip in terms of ounces, and train dispensers to scoop accurate portions every time.

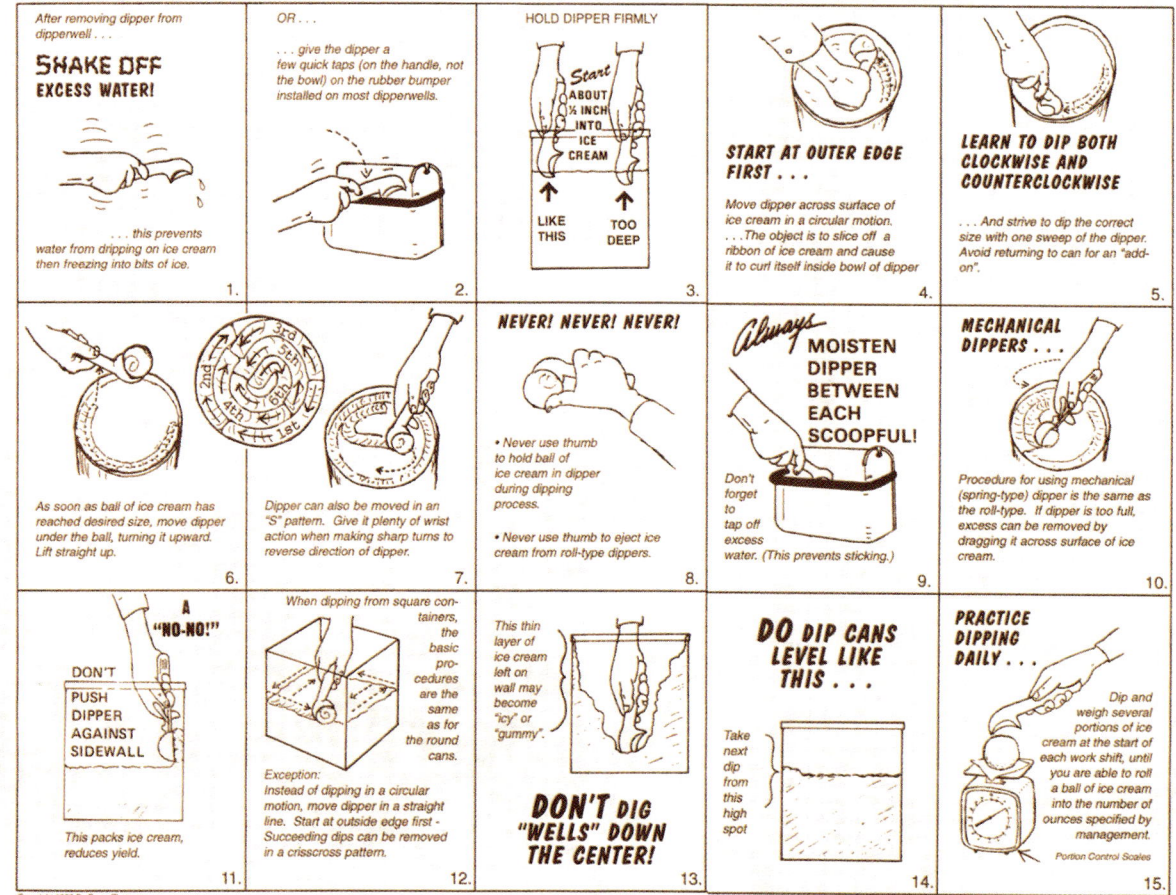

Ice Cream Joe: THE VALLEY DAIRY STORY

The grand opening of the new Valley Dairy Restaurant in Blairsville, Pennsylvania, October 2004. Joe and Virginia Greubel managed to collect only three of their nine grandchildren for the event. Left to right: Virginia Greubel, Kevin Blystone, Joe Greubel (in uniform), Alex "Ice Cream Alex" Blystone, Melissa Blystone, Lindsay Blystone, and Mary Jo Sell.

Though ice cream retailers feared that their business would suffer when Prohibition was repealed in the early 1930s, Joe Greubel was born too late to have to worry about it. Here he is in Germany, sampling the local brew and deciding what to order from an ice cream menu.

Carl Mattioli, President of the Latrobe Historical Society, and Joe E. Greubel in a promo shot for the 2004 celebration of the invention of the banana split. Carl holds an original banana split dish that Dr. Strickler had custom made at a Jeannette glass factory. Joe holds an early Valley Dairy ice cream scoop. Between them is the airmail pickup bag used in the world's first official airmail pickup at Latrobe Airport, May 1938.

Ice Cream Joe: THE VALLEY DAIRY STORY

Joe E. Greubel in a 1961 photo serving guests at a buffet for a Latrobe business breakfast. Left to right: Latrobe Mayor Victor E. Stader; Harold Paul, local jeweler; "Pat" Lennon, Kennametal vice-president. Joe serves Bill Maccarelli of Kamp's Shoes, while attorney Henry Mahady and Harry Whiteman of the Latrobe Bulletin await their turn.

Joe E. Greubel at a Reinhart food show at Seven Springs Resort, Somerset, Pennsylvania. He poses with some the the staff.

Joe E. Greubel (in the Derby hat) promotes "red hots" at one of the first Valley Dairy stores in Latrobe.

A clerk serves a cone at the original Valley Dairy at 313 Main Street, Latrobe.

Ice Cream Joe: THE VALLEY DAIRY STORY

SOME SPECIAL ADS AND PROMOS

Left: Three of the early ads Joe F. Greubel placed in the local newspapers. Over the years, when daughter-in-law Virginia took over the advertising end of the Valley Dairy business, Valley Dairy ads grew in sophistication.

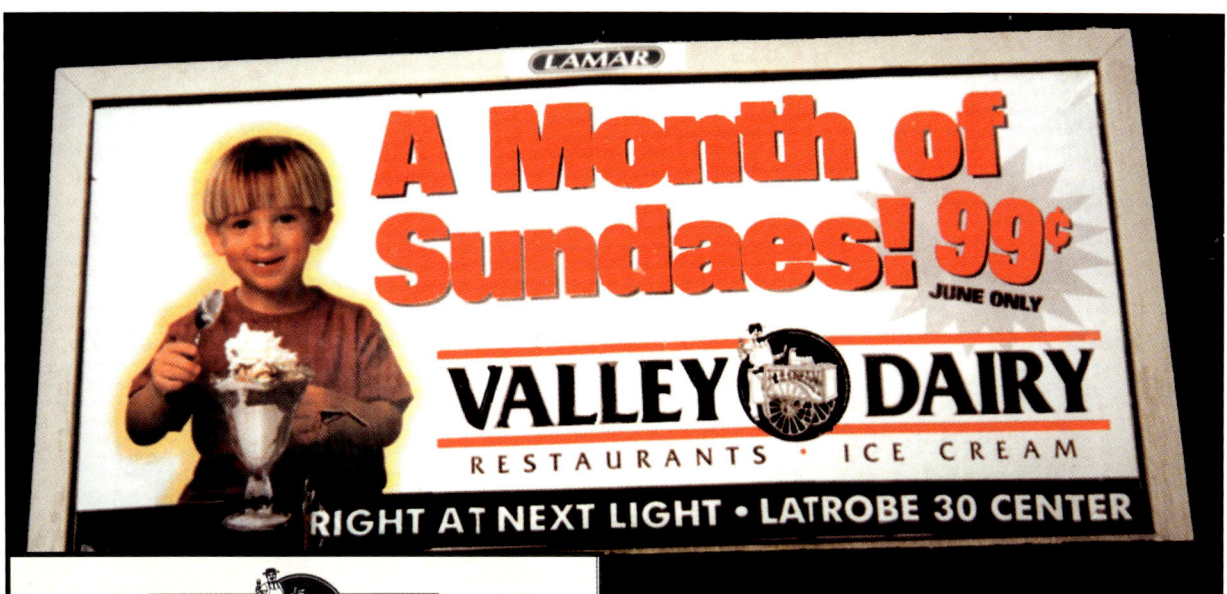

Ice Cream Joe: THE VALLEY DAIRY STORY

If I Look Smug—It's Because I'm So Pleased With Our New Container

It's hard to be humble when we have so much to be proud of at Valley Dairy! Our bright, new red and white ice cream container may be different on the outside but the same high quality ice cream that's been our trademark for almost a century is still the same inside. Look for our new Valley Dairy ice cream carton in our stores or in many supermarkets. It's our Pleasin' Season at Valley Dairy and we want an opportunity to please you, so stop in soon.

Ice Cream Joe

VALLEY DAIRY
- 1419 Ligonier St.
- Cor. Jefferson & Chestnut St.
- Latrobe 30 Shopping Plaza

Valley Dairy and Fort Ligonier manager, Dick Bittner, sponsored this event at the Valley Dairy in the Richland Shopping Center in Johnstown, Pennsylvania. The event was held to encourage the public to attend the annual Fort Ligonier Days. The Seneca Indians in Chief Grey Wolf's troupe provided the dancing. Fort Ligonier was prominent in the French and Indian War.

Ice Cream Joe: THE VALLEY DAIRY STORY

THE BIG FIRES...

Joe E. Greubel inspects fire damage in the second-floor apartment where the fire apparently started. "You never fully realize the benefit and impact of volunteer firemen until you have a situation like this. It really makes you appreciate those people. It's a good thing they are volunteers. No one could ever pay enough for their services," commented Greubel.

DAMAGE SET AT $75,000

NOVEMBER 21, 1996
FROM THE INDEPENDENT
Jim Gallagher

A Ligonier Street apartment building was badly damaged by fire Monday, which caused an estimated $75,000 in damage.

"It started on a couch in the living room of a second-floor apartment," said Latrobe VFD Chief John Orzehowski. "We're not sure exactly what started the fire, but we don't believe it was a cigarette butt."

Fairview Dairy, parent company of Valley Dairy, which has an office on the first floor, owns the building.

At one point, the fire also looked like it might spread to the adjacent S&H Electric Building. When firemen arrived on the scene, an S&H employee was on the roof of his building with a garden hose, spraying at flames that were licking the side of the structure from a second-floor apartment.

Firemen on the scene

Fred Kimmick, employee of S&H Electric Supply battles the Valley Dairy blaze from an adjacent rooftop with a garden hose.

Valley Dairy was the victim of a second fire in downtown Latrobe. An unidentified dog lends a supportive eye to the firefighters.

Ice Cream Joe: THE VALLEY DAIRY STORY

HOLIDAY INN: PITTSBURGH FIRSTS PROMO 2004

Soda jerk Joe Greubel prepares banana splits for splits for all.

A promotion for "Area Firsts" highlights the Greater Pittsburgh Airport's Holiday Inn's promotions for 2004. The invention of the banana split by Dr. David Strickler in 1904 in Latrobe is included on the agenda, along with other "firsts" like KDKA and the nation's first radio broadcast, and the nation's first professional football game which occurred in Latrobe.

Top left to right: Cathy Brant of Mountain View Inn, Latrobe, Pennsylvania; Andy Stofan, Latrobe Chamber of Commerce, Tom Lazarchik, last owner of Strickler's Drug Store, where the banana split was invented in 1904.

Right: Joe E. Greubel, and Don Orlando, Public Relations Director at Saint Vincent College.

Don Orlando and Joe Greubel at the Banana split bar.

Ice Cream Joe: THE VALLEY DAIRY STORY

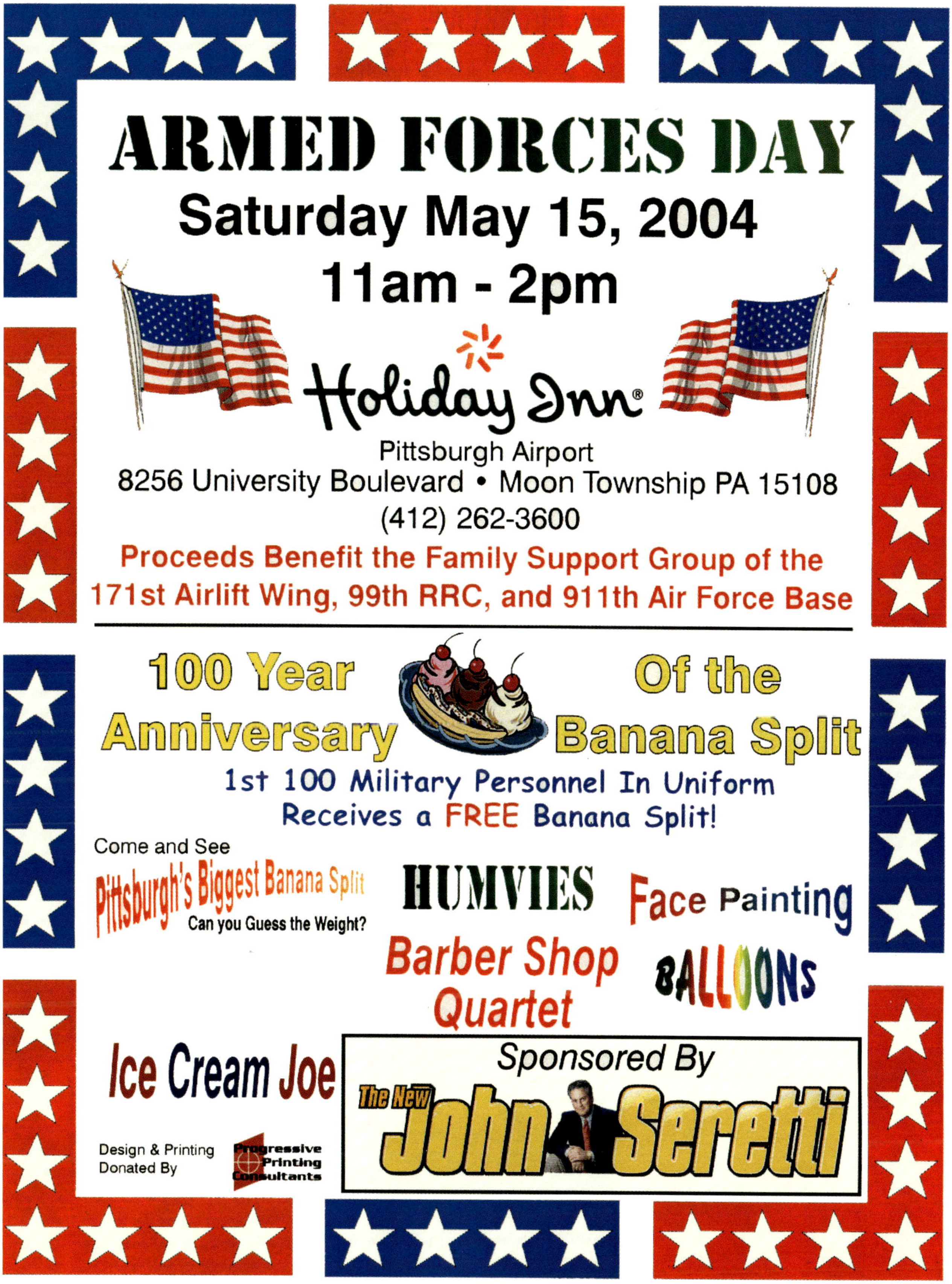
ARMED FORCES DAY
Saturday May 15, 2004
11am - 2pm
Holiday Inn®
Pittsburgh Airport
8256 University Boulevard • Moon Township PA 15108
(412) 262-3600
Proceeds Benefit the Family Support Group of the
171st Airlift Wing, 99th RRC, and 911th Air Force Base
100 Year Anniversary Of the Banana Split
1st 100 Military Personnel In Uniform
Receives a FREE Banana Split!
Come and See
Pittsburgh's Biggest Banana Split
Can you Guess the Weight?
HUMVIES
Face Painting
Barber Shop Quartet
BALLOONS
Ice Cream Joe
Sponsored By
The New John Seretti
Design & Printing Donated By
Progressive Printing Consultants

May 15, 2004 - The Holiday Inn "Armed Forces Day" promo. Top: Three-year-old Mia Bennett digs into a banana split.

Joe E. Greubel and "The Love Bug". . . Carla the Clown pose before a monumental, 307-pound banana split.

EDITOR'S NOTE

The Saint Vincent College Center for Northern Appalachian Studies extends its thanks to the following who, through their support and direct contributions, helped to make this history possible: Joseph E. Greubel, who saved just about everything in a "highly organized" filing system. Without Joe's material, this history of his family's business would not have been possible; Virginia Greubel, Joe's wife, whose filing system is rivaled only by Joe's; Joe's daughters, Melissa and Mary Jo. Special thanks to J.S. Downs and Associates; Rebecca Humrich of Sheridan Books, Don Orlando and the Public Relations department at Saint Vincent College; Patty Dellinger (College Business office), Shirley Skander (College Faculty Secretary), Lee Ann Ross (College's Mailing and Duplicating department), and Donna Werner (College Post Office), who, for the thirteen years since the Center was founded, have been there with unselfish, timely, and patient assistance.

ACKNOWLEDGEMENTS

I never realized that publishing a book could be such a time-consuming project, nor that it would require the assistance of so many. I don't know how I will be able to remember and thank everyone who helped.

First of all, I give a special thanks to Professor Richard Wissolik of Saint Vincent College, his wife Barbara, and the staff at the college's Center for Northern Appalachian Studies. They worked through what seemed like a truckload of material to produce this book. Thanks to Don Orlando, the Public Relations Director at Saint Vincent College; Carl Mattioli, President of the Latrobe Historical Society; Bryce Thomson, the World's Greatest Soda Jerk and Editor of the Sundae School Newsletter. Bryce has been a close, family friend over the years; Ed Marks, Founder of the Ice Screamers and author of Ice Cream Collectibles; Michael Turback, author of the Banana Split Book and A Month of Sundaes. Thanks to all of the past and present fellow members of the National Ice Cream Retailers Association, especially Jim Norris and Henry Gentry.

Thanks to all who contributed a story and/or a photograph. Thanks to Reverend David McCracken; my wife Virginia; my daughters, Margaret, Melissa and Mary Jo. Thanks Tom Greubel, Mary Agnes McGinnis, Janet Hudson, Tom Himler, Chester College, Bill Hughes, Dick Myers, Tom Lazarchik, Ray Sheets, Bill Dymond, and Bob Williams. Thanks to all of the mentors and sales people who helped our family business over the years. Thanks to all of our present and past employees. Thanks to our customers.

I know Dad would say thanks to you. He knew that our customers were our greatest assets, and we value you more than words can express. You will always be "Our Favorite Flavor!"

Sincerely

Ice Cream Joe

Joseph E. Greubel
Ice Cream Joe

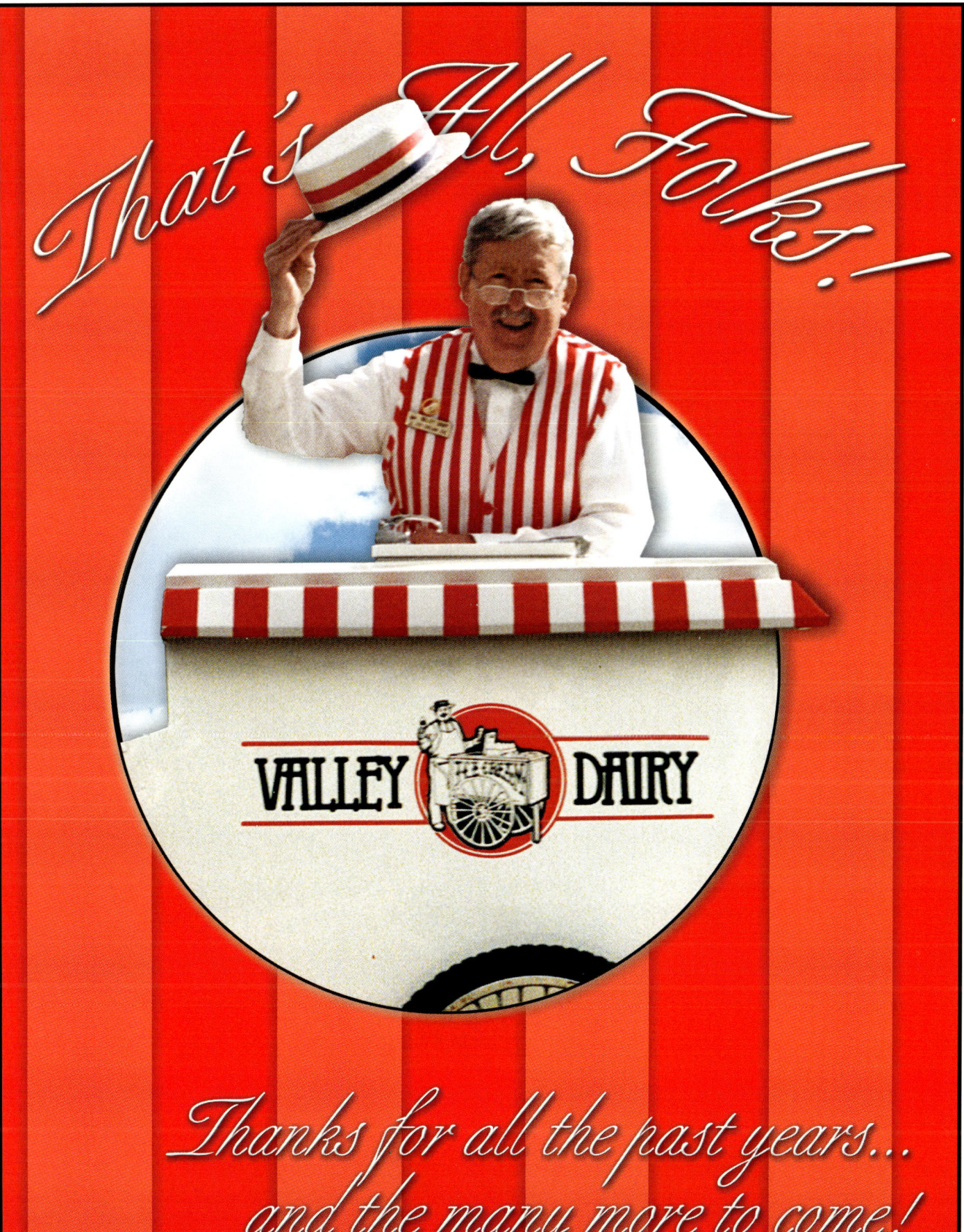

SOURCES AND BIBLIOGRAPHY

Alexander, Eleanor. "A Uniquely American Watering Hole: The Drug Store Soda Fountain at the Turn of the Century." Master's Thesis: University of Delaware, 1986.

American Soda Fountain Co. *The American Soda Book*. Boston, d.n.a.

Beamon, Sylvia P. *The Ice Houses of Britain*. Routledge, 1990.

Belden, Louise Conway. *The Festive Tradition: Table Decoration and Desserts in America, 1650–1900*. New York: WW Norton, 1983.

Buxham, Tim. *Icehouses*. Shire: 1992, rp. 1998.

Cummings, Richard O. *The American Ice Harvests: An Historical Study in Technology, 1800–1918*. Berkeley and Los Angeles: U of California Press, 1949.

Dairy Queen International. *The Cone with the Curl on Top: Celebrating Fifty Years, 1940–1990*. Minneapolis, 1990.

Damerow, Gail. *Ice Cream: The Whole Scoop*. Macomb, Illinois: Glenbridge Publishing, 1991.

David, Elizabeth. *Harvest of the Cold Months. The Social History of Ice and Ices*. Joseph, 1994.

Dispenser's Formulary or Soda Water Guide. Third ed., rev. New York: Haynes, 1915.

Eales, Mrs. Mary. *Receipts* [Recipes] London: Prospect Books, 1733.

Dickson, Paul. *The Great American Ice Cream Book*. Absolute Press, 1984.

Funderburg, Ann Cooper. *Chocolate, Strawberry & Vanilla*. Bowling Green U. Popular Press, 1995.

Hall, Henry. *The Ice Cream Industry of the United States with a Brief Sketch of Its History and Estimates of Production in the Different States*. Washington, D..C.: Government Printing House, 1888.

Howard Johnson's. *Howard Johnson's Presents Old Time Ice Cream Soda Fountain Recipes or How to Make a Soda Fountain Pay*. New York: Winter House, 1971.

Ice Cream Merchandising Institute, Inc. *Let's Sell Ice Cream*. Washington, D.C., 1947.

Ice Cream Review. Issues 1900s to Mid-Century. Complete series extant in the Greubel Archives.

Ice Cream Trade Journal. Trade Paper Division of the Reuben Donnelley Corp. Philadelphia.

International Association of Ice Cream Manufacturers. *The History of Ice Cream*.

Jones, Joseph C. *America's Icemen: An Illustrated History of the United States Natural Ice Industry, 1665–1925*. Humble, Texas: Jobeco Books, 1984.

Jones, Thomas P. *Ice Cream World of Baskin-Robbins*. New York: Pinnacle Books, 1975.

Lager, Fred. *Ben and Jerry's: The Inside Scoop*. New York: Coward-McCann, 1994.

Marks, Ed. *Ice Cream Collectibles*. Atglen, PA: Schiffer Books, 2003.

Marshall, A.B. *The Book of Ices*. London: Marshall's, 1885.

Miller, Val. *Thirty-six Years and Ice Cream Maker: Receipts and Pointers*. Davenport, Iowa, 1907.

The National Dipper: The Magazine for Frozen Dessert Retailers. Lynda Utterback, Publisher and Editor. Published six times a year. Rolling Meadows, Illinois.

National Ice Cream Retailers Association [N.I.C.R.A.] *Yearbooks and Bulletins*.

Palmer, Carl J. *History of the Soda Fountain Industry*. Washington, D.C.: Soda Fountain Manufacturers' Association, 1947.

Paul, Charlie. *American and Other Iced Drinks*. London: Farrow and Jackson, 1909.

Pomeroy, Ralph. *The Ice Cream Connection*. Paddington Press, 1975.

Selitzer, Ralph. *The Dairy Industry in America*. New York Magazines for Industry, 1976.

Senn,, Herman C. *Luncheon and Dinner Sweets Including the Art of Ice Making*. Ward Lock, 1910.

Smith, Wayne. Ice Cream Dippers: *An Illustrated History and Collector's Guide to Early Ice Cream Dippers*. Walkersville, MD: Wayne Smith, 1986.

Stallings, W.S., Jr. "Ice Cream and Water Ices in the Seventeenth and Eighteenth Centuries." *Petits Propos Culinaires*. 3 November, 1979.

Stogo, Malcolm. *Frozen Desserts: A Complete Retailer's Guide*. New York: Van Nostrand Reinhold, 1991.

The Ice Creamer. Collectibles. Published Quarterly. 1982-present.

Turback, Michael. *The Banana Split Book: Everything There is to Know about America's Greatest Dessert*. Philadelphia: Camino Books, 2004.

Turnbow, Grover Dean, Paul Tracy, Lloyd Raffeto. *The Ice Cream Industry*. New York: Wiley, 1947.

AUTOGRAPHS

Ice Cream Joe: THE VALLEY DAIRY STORY